Selected Works of Elinor Wylie

Selected Works of Elinor Wylie

Edited and with an Introduction
by Evelyn Helmick Hively

The Kent State University Press
KENT, OHIO

Library of Congress Catalog Card Number 2004028270
ISBN-10: 0-87338-829-1
ISBN-13: 978-0-87338-829-0
Manufactured in the United States of America

09 08 07 06 05 5 4 3 2 1

LIBRARY OF CONGRESS CATALOGING-IN-PUBLICATION DATA
Wylie, Elinor, 1885–1928.
[Selections. 2005]
Selected works of Elinor Wylie / edited and with an introduction by Evelyn Helmick Hively.
p. cm.
Includes index.
ISBN 0-87338-829-1 (pbk. : alk. paper) ∞
I. Hively, Evelyn Helmick. II. Title.
PS3545.Y45A6 2005
811'.52—dc22 2004028270

British Library Cataloging-in-Publication data are available.

Contents

Introduction

At the height of Elinor Wylie's fame, Carl Van Doren, Columbia University professor and editor of the *Century,* called her "the queen of poets"; Edmund Wilson, the reigning critic, marveled at her "almost supernatural brilliance and energy." Her poems and stories were published in *Poetry, Vanity Fair,* the *New Republic,* the *New Yorker,* and other leading magazines of the day. Her four volumes of poetry and four novels written from 1921 to 1928 were all best-selling books.

With the exception of a few frequently anthologized poems, the work of Elinor Wylie is not often remembered today. The reputations of most of the leading women poets who were celebrated in the 1920s suffered in the later decades of the century, but Wylie's light dimmed earliest and most dramatically.

Today, entries in encyclopedias of women writers say more about Wylie's provocative personality and unconventional life than about her work. The collected poems have not been reissued since their first publication in 1932. Still, authoritative voices of contemporary criticism express interest in her poetry. Rebecca West considered Wylie a writer who "has slipped out of sight while her inferiors have been over-remembered." Noting the current neglect of the female writers of the twenties, Clive James added, "but, when you look at the work of Elinor Wylie, in particular, it is astonishing how accomplished she was." John Gordan, former curator at the Berg Collection of the New York Public Library, predicted that she would return to public attention.

There is no denying that her beauty, social status, and behavior add interest to her poetry and fiction, which so often make direct references to herself. The people who knew her and the population at large seemed as preoccupied with the events of her life as she was. Their interest extended to her equally fascinating family, the "mad Hoyts," as the newspapers called them. Elinor Wylie's father, Henry Hoyt, was assistant attorney general and later solicitor general in the administrations of McKinley, Roosevelt, and Taft, and his children enjoyed lives of affluence and prominence in Washington society. But when Hoyt died suddenly at the age of fifty-three in 1910, the family began to disintegrate. Elinor almost immediately left her husband, Philip Hichborn, and their three-year-old son to flee to England with Horace Wylie, an older married man and the father of three children; a brother and a sister were suicides, as was her husband; a younger brother and sister started their descent into alcoholism and early death.

For six years in villages of southern England, Elinor Hoyt Hichborn read and studied with the remarkably well-educated Horace Wylie, who encouraged her interest in writing poetry and arranged for the anonymously published *Incidental Numbers.* They returned to America with the threat of war and, on their return to Washington, were ostracized in spite of their eventual marriage in 1916. At this time, Elinor Wylie began to write poetry in earnest, and the periodicals of the day were eager to print them. She was helped in her publishing ventures by William Rose Benét, who had been her brother's friend at Yale and would become her mentor and agent, her lover, and eventually her third husband. With the exception of a few early poems, all of her work was written during her relationship with this talented, loving, and supportive man of literature.

The four volumes of poetry that Wylie produced in the decade before her death in 1928—*Nets to Catch the Wind, Black Armour, Trivial Breath,* and *Angels and Earthly Creatures*—trace a remarkable literary career that seemed to critics to be fully developed from the start. But she had begun to write poems while she was still in school, according to a classmate who had read her sonnet titled "Fear." The romantic themes and conventional forms in the privately published *Incidental Numbers,* a slight volume of twenty-five poems, presage her mature work. She chose only two of those early poems dated from 1902 to 1911, however, for later publication.

By 1921 Wylie had enough poems for her first signed collection, *Nets to Catch the Wind.* Her claim that all of the poems had been previously published was not quite true; nineteen of the thirty-one poems in that book had appeared in *Poetry,* the *New Republic,* the *Nation,* the *Bookman,* and other major journals. Edna St. Vincent Millay, the first reviewer of the volume, praised the author's "intelligence, skill, discrimination, reserve, and full powers of sorcery." She especially liked the poem "Atavism" and the sonnet sequence "Wild Peaches." Years later William Butler Yeats wrote privately to his sister that "The Eagle and the Mole," a "lovely heroic song," was his sole excitement at the time. *Nets to Catch the Wind* was a surprising success, winning the Poetry Society's prize for the best book of poetry published in 1921.

Wylie said that she had sold all of the poems in her next volume to periodicals before they appeared as *Black Armour.* In this title, as elsewhere, she chose the British spelling and sometimes the locution over the American, undoubtedly prompted by her six years in England studying literature and by her constant reading of the Romantics and other British writers. William Rose Benét wrote that the collection, which was dedicated to him, was full of poems very personal to the couple. Those references are important in reading the poems, as is the move from the escapist themes of *Nets to Catch the Wind* to a more defensive posture. The era of the twenties valued defenses in the forms of wit, masks, and surfaces that could not be penetrated. *Black Armour* suggests self-protection and even battle. "Let No Charitable Hope," sent to Benét to settle a quarrel, is representative of the poems of that volume.

Before she gathered material for her third signed volume of poetry, Wylie published four novels at the suggestion of Sinclair Lewis, who persuaded her that writing fiction was the way to earn money. *Jennifer Lorn: A Sedate Extravaganza* is the story of a beautiful, aristocratic eighteenth-century English girl and her adventures with three men in France, India, and Persia. There is not, as Harriet Monroe said, a trace of reality anywhere in the concoction, but there are exotic places, baroque objets d'art, eccentric characters, and funny twists of plot. Lewis sent his approval: "At last, a civilized American novel"; and the novelist Carl Van Vechten led a torchlight parade in New York to celebrate its publication.

The Venetian Glass Nephew, Wylie's second novel, set in eighteenth-century Italy, is the fantastic tale of an evil glass blower who creates a "nephew" for Cardinal Peter Innocent Bon, who promptly marries him to a natural daughter of another cardinal. Their alliance creates the metaphor for Wylie's observations on art versus nature, and the Italian scenes provide descriptions of art, religion, and magic. The critic Joseph Wood Krutch wrote that in this novel Elinor Wylie had disclosed the precise moment in the Renaissance that Christian sensibility fused with paganism. Most reviewers described *The Venetian Glass Nephew* as "fantasy," but Wylie rejected the word as lacking dignity; for all of her novels she preferred "allegory." In her work, allegory often heightens the satire that is always present.

Another narrative of the eighteenth century, *The Orphan Angel,* begins with the rescue of Shelley during the storm in Leghorn Harbor and his transport to America, where he searches the western wilderness for the lovely Silver Cross, one of Wylie's alter egos. The dialog between Shiloh, the aristocratic Shelleyan figure, and Davy Butternut, a simple American, allows lively comparisons between cultures. The religious tone is clear, and as Donald Pizer points out, the plot is a modern grail quest. Wylie's lifelong obsession with Shelley and his work made the creation of *The Orphan Angel* her own spiritual journey.

In *Mr. Hodge and Mr. Hazard* Wylie created a composite of Romantic poets to form the character of Mr. Hazard, who is also, by her own admission,

Wylie herself. In nineteenth-century England, he is an idealist of great sensitivity who is not understood by modern society. Reviewers found in this novel social significance, an interesting study in psychology, and a "rhapsody in words." Like all of Wylie's novels it is a poet's experiment in prose. She preferred to call it a "brief symbolic romance of the mind."

She returned to poetry with *Trivial Breath,* released at about the same time as *Mr. Hodge and Mr. Hazard.* The four-sonnet sequence, "Dedication," and several of the best poems in the volume—"A Red Carpet for Shelley," "Lament for Glasgerion," and "Tragic Dialogue"—are testaments to Elinor Wylie's worship of Shelley. Like many of the other poems in this collection, they speak of mortality in tragic tones. In these poems, too, she shows mastery of her craft and freer, more confident rhythms. The editors of *Poetry* awarded her the Levinson Prize of 1928 for *Trivial Breath.*

In *Angels and Earthly Creatures* Wylie's art rose to its peak with poems that demonstrated the full measure of her talent. The nineteen poems of the "One Person" sonnet sequence, with their theme of love and death, were declared by her contemporaries to be close to Shakespeare and among the best love poems in any language. The sonnets were inspired by a married Englishman to whom Elinor Wylie was attracted during the last year of her life. The most important of the other poems in the volume—"Hymn to Earth," "This Corruptible," "O Virtuous Light,"—are spiritual and profound, the result of the same heightened poetic power that she believed her love had created.

Elinor Wylie carefully selected and arranged the poems in *Angels and Earthly Creatures* just before she died, undoubtedly aware that this was the final volume of poetry that she controlled. When William Rose Benét published the *Collected Poems of Elinor Wylie* a few years later, he included a section called "Hitherto Unpublished Poems." Most interesting of those are "Pretty Words" and "Doomsday" for their demonstration of Wylie's virtuosity and "For a Good Girl" and "For a Good Boy" for their revelations of her relationships with Dorothy Parker and Sir George Young. One pleasure of the book is Benét's foreword, which, along with his "Prose and Poetry of Elinor Wylie," a lecture published by Wheaton College Press, summarizes his valuable personal and professional analysis of her work. In 1943 he authorized the publication of *Last Poems of Elinor Wylie,* with some new pieces transcribed by Jane Wise and a tribute by Edith Olivier. The poems of interest include the biographical "Beltane" and "Silver Bells and Cockle Shells," the early "Written on the Flyleaf of John Webster's Plays," and "From the Wall," often cited by today's feminist readers. "Last Poems" is a misleading title, meaning only the last Wylie work published; the collection bears little resemblance to the poems that she wrote last, truly her best.

Her poetry and prose as a whole can be read as an autobiography written during the 1920s, a narrative that reveals much about the attitudes and manners of the time as well as the development of Wylie as a writer and a woman. From the beauty with a "hard heart of a child" in the first poem of *Nets To Catch the Wind* to the spiritual maturity of "Hymn to Earth" in *Angels and Earthly Creatures,* she questions herself, argues with herself, accuses herself; then she provides the difficult, harshly honest answers in her poetry that she so seldom managed in her life. Some poems, like "Peter and John," provide a surprise ending; some, like "Hughie at the Inn," make a final witty refutation of what has gone before; some are confessional explications. But all end by facing the truth, however painful. Even the *New Yorker* poem, "A Portrait in Black Paint," as flippant as it seems, is a probing examination of Wylie's character—so devastatingly so that readers wrote to denounce the author, who had signed only her initials. Her poems ranged from the playful, like "Little Joke," to the tragic, like "Farewell, Sweet Dust." Even within a poem, she can, as one critic has said, "be completely simple in one breath and murderously complex in the next." Much of her strength lies in her struggle to find the truth of any situation through poetic analysis. The end is a brutal honesty that refuses to avoid reality, as in the early "Sea Lullaby," with its ironic title and the bitter accusation of nature as a murderer, or in "Little Elegy," with its denial of those symbols of nature that soften grief in most elegies, and its acceptance of total desolation in loss.

Her four novels record the same personal development, from the young girl who experienced relationships with several men in *Jennifer Lorn,* to the transformation she underwent in *A Venetian Glass Nephew,* through the various personas that she tried on to please her hero in *The Orphan Angel,* and finally to the aging author who wished only to withdraw from an unsympathetic world. About a writer who kept no journal and who revealed little of her life in her letters, we learn much from her poems and her novels. All of her work springs from her search for identity and the desperate attempt to maintain it in difficult circumstances.

Her achievement to some degree must be credited to Wylie's intense devotion to her art through illness, emotional stress, and what she called "a sky reversed and evil-starred." The wide variety of her forms, the mastery of the sonnet that produced "One Person," often considered one of the great sonnet sequences in English, her exact rhythms and word choices—all delight and finally instruct. Careful study of Wylie's poems confirms the judgment of some critics that she is the most intellectual of the women poets of the twenties. A *New York Times* review of her *Collected Prose* in 1933 quotes a critic who says that appreciation for Elinor Wylie is a gauge of one's education, and continues,

"Certainly she requires much of the reader." Her contribution to literature, then, is more than a supreme poetic technique and a mastery of language. She brilliantly dissects the elements of identity, illuminating ways to understand the self. What she said of Yeats's readers is true of hers as well: everyone will in some measure see the image of himself in its crystal.

The poems in this book are printed as they appear in *The Collected Poems of Elinor Wylie* (New York: Knopf, 1932), and the novels and shorter pieces are from *The Collected Prose of Elinor Wylie* (New York: Knopf, 1933). The publication of those volumes was directed by Wylie's third husband, William Rose Benét, after her death. He consistently chose the British spelling and syntax that she had always preferred and routinely used after her years in England but that earlier editors at other publishing houses had often changed in editions of the individual poetry collections and novels.

The date and place of first publication for each entry, when known, appear just after the title. That information reveals her appeal among the readers of the popular literary journals of her time, as well as among the novel readers in England and the United States. The dates also make apparent her extraordinary creativity in just eight years of professional writing. The development of her literary powers during those years is an interesting study in itself, and this time frame elucidates the close relationship of her work to the events of her life.

In the selection of both poetry and prose for this volume, emphasis has been first on the remarkable range of Wylie's intellect and literary skill and then on the ideas and attitudes that will interest contemporary readers. As she said, "There's sorcery in it, and surprise."

Poetry

Sea-blue Eyes

By ELINOR WYLIE

I stare at you, Ianthe, since you ask,
Because your eyes look, brimmed with fervid blue,
Like disks of crystal in a tinted mask
Which the intense Ægean gazes through.

Century 102, no. 264 (June 1921).

CHAPTER ONE

From *Incidental Numbers*

London: William Clowes and Sons, 1912

The Knight Fallen on Evil Days

Saturday Review of Literature, April 1927

God send the Devil is a gentleman
Else had I none amongst mine enemies!
O what uncouth and cruel times are these
In which the unlettered Boor and Artisan,
The snarling Priest and smirking Lawyer can
Spit filthy enmity at whom they please—
At one, returned from spilling overseas
The Princely blood of foes Olympian.

Apothecaries curse me, who of late
Was cursed by Kings for slaughtering French lords!
Friendless and loverless is my estate,
Yet God be praised that Hell at least affords
An adversary worthy of my hate,
With whom the Angels deigned to measure swords!

Pegasus Lost

Untermeyer, *Modern American Poetry*

And there I found a gray and ancient ass,
With dull glazed stare, and stubborn wrinkled smile,
Sardonic, mocking my wide-eyed amaze,
A clumsy hulking form in that white place
At odds with the small stable, cleanly, Greek,
The marble manger and the golden oats.
With loathing hands I felt the ass's side,
Solidly real and hairy to the touch.
Then knew I that I dreamed not, but saw truth;
And knowing, wished I still might hope I dreamed.
The door stood wide, I went into the air.
The day was blue and filled with rushing wind,
A day to ride high in the heavens and taste
The glory of the gods who tread the stars.
Up in the mighty purity I saw
A flashing shape that gladly sprang aloft—
My little Pegasus, like a far white bird
Seeking sun-regions, never to return.
Silently then I turned my steps about,
Entered the stable, saddled the slow ass;
Then on its back I journeyed dustily
Between sun-wilted hedgerows into town.

"Les Lauriers Sont Coupés"

Contemporary Verse, May 1920

Ah, love, within the shadow of the wood
The laurels are cut down; some other brows
May bear the classic wreath which Fame allows
And find the burden honorable and good.
Have we not passed the laurels as they stood—
Soft in the veil with which the Spring endows
The wintry glitter of their woven boughs—
Nor stopped to break the branches while we could?

Ah, love, for other brows they are cut down.
Thornless and scentless are their stems and flowers,
And cold as death their twisted coronal.
Sweeter to us the sharpness of this crown;
Sweeter the wildest roses which are ours;
Sweeter the petals, even when they fall.

CHAPTER TWO

From *Nets to Catch the Wind*

New York: Harcourt Brace and Company, 1921
London: Alfred A. Knopf, 1928
Collected Poems of Elinor Wylie. New York: Alfred A. Knopf, 1932

Beauty

New York Evening Post, October 1920

Say not of Beauty she is good,
Or aught but beautiful,
Or sleek to doves' wings of the wood
Her wild wings of a gull.

Call her not wicked; that word's touch
Consumes her like a curse;
But love her not too much, too much,
For that is even worse.

O, she is neither good nor bad,
But innocent and wild!
Enshrine her and she dies, who had
The hard heart of a child.

The Eagle and the Mole

New Republic, January 1921
Bookman, April 1921

Avoid the reeking herd,
Shun the polluted flock,
Live like that stoic bird,
The eagle of the rock.

The huddled warmth of crowds
Begets and fosters hate;
He keeps, above the clouds,
His cliff inviolate.

When flocks are folded warm,
And herds to shelter run,
He sails above the storm,
He stares into the sun.

If in the eagle's track
Your sinews cannot leap,
Avoid the lathered pack,
Turn from the steaming sheep.

If you would keep your soul
From spotted sight or sound,
Live like the velvet mole;
Go burrow underground.

And there hold intercourse
With roots of trees and stones,
With rivers at their source,
And disembodied bones.

Madman's Song

Century, October 1920
Current Opinion, April 1922

Better to see your cheek grown hollow,
Better to see your temple worn,
Than to forget to follow, follow,
After the sound of a silver horn.

Better to bind your brow with willow
And follow, follow until you die,
Than to sleep with your head on golden pillow,
Nor lift it up when the hunt goes by.

Better to see your cheek grown sallow
And your hair grown gray, so soon, so soon,
Than to forget to hallo, hallo,
After the milk-white hounds of the moon.

August

New Republic, August 1920

Why should this Negro insolently stride
Down the red noonday on such noiseless feet?
Piled in his barrow, tawnier than wheat,
Lie heaps of smoldering daisies, sombre-eyed,
Their copper petals shrivelled up with pride,
Hot with a superfluity of heat,
Like a great brazier borne along the street
By captive leopards, black and burning pied.

Are there no water-lilies, smooth as cream,
With long stems dripping crystal? Are there none
Like those white lilies, luminous and cool,
Plucked from some hemlock-darkened northern stream
By fair-haired swimmers, diving where the sun
Scarce warms the surface of the deepest pool?

The Crooked Stick

First Traveller: What's that lying in the dust?
Second Traveller: A crooked stick.
First Traveller: What's it worth, if you can trust
        To arithmetic?
Second Traveller: Isn't this a riddle?
First Traveller: No, a trick.
Second Traveller: It's worthless. Leave it where it lies.
First Traveller: Wait; count ten;
        Rub a little dust upon your eyes;
        Now, look again.
Second Traveller: Well, and what the devil is it, then?
First Traveller: It's the sort of crooked stick that shepherds know.
Second Traveller: Someone's loss!
First Traveller: Bend it, and you make of it a bow.
Break it, a cross.
Second Traveller: But it's all grown over with moss!

Atavism

Poetry, April 1920

I always was afraid of Somes's Pond:
Not the little pond, by which the willow stands,
Where laughing boys catch alewives in their hands
In brown, bright shallows; but the one beyond.
There, when the frost makes all the birches burn
Yellow as cow-lilies, and the pale sky shines
Like a polished shell between black spruce and pines,
Some strange thing tracks us, turning where we turn.

You'll say I dream it, being the true daughter
Of those who in old times endured this dread.
Look! Where the lily-stems are showing red
A silent paddle moves below the water,
A sliding shape has stirred them like a breath;
Tall plumes surmount a painted mask of death.

Wild Peaches

1

When the world turns completely upside down
You say we'll emigrate to the Eastern Shore
Aboard a river-boat from Baltimore;
We'll live among wild peach trees, miles from town,
You'll wear a coonskin cap, and I a gown
Homespun, dyed butternut's dark gold colour.
Lost, like your lotus-eating ancestor,
We'll swim in milk and honey till we drown.

The winter will be short, the summer long,
The autumn amber-hued, sunny and hot,
Tasting of cider and of scuppernong;
All seasons sweet, but autumn best of all.
The squirrels in their silver fur will fall
Like falling leaves, like fruit, before your shot.

2

The autumn frosts will lie upon the grass
Like bloom on grapes of purple-brown and gold.
The misted early mornings will be cold;
The little puddles will be roofed with glass.
The sun, which burns from copper into brass,
Melts these at noon, and makes the boys unfold
Their knitted mufflers; full as they can hold,
Fat pockets dribble chestnuts as they pass.

Peaches grow wild, and pigs can live in clover;
A barrel of salted herrings lasts a year;
The spring begins before the winter's over.
By February you may find the skins
Of garter snakes and water moccasins
Dwindled and harsh, dead-white and cloudy-clear.

3

When April pours the colours of a shell
Upon the hills, when every little creek

Is shot with silver from the Chesapeake
In shoals new-minted by the ocean swell,
When strawberries go begging, and the sleek
Blue plums lie open to the blackbird's beak,
We shall live well—we shall live very well.

The months between the cherries and the peaches
Are brimming cornucopias which spill
Fruits red and purple, sombre-bloomed and black;
Then, down rich fields and frosty river beaches
We'll trample bright persimmons, while you kill
Bronze partridge, speckled quail, and canvasback.

4

Down to the Puritan marrow of my bones
There's something in this richness that I hate.
I love the look, austere, immaculate,
Of landscapes drawn in pearly monotones.
There's something in my very blood that owns
Bare hills, cold silver on a sky of slate,
A thread of water, churned to milky spate
Streaming through slanted pastures fenced with stones.

I love those skies, thin blue or snowy gray,
Those fields sparse-planted, rendering meagre sheaves;
That spring, briefer than apple-blossom's breath,
Summer, so much too beautiful to stay,
Swift autumn, like a bonfire of leaves,
And sleepy winter, like the sleep of death.

Sanctuary

This is the bricklayer; hear the thud
Of his heavy load dumped down on stone.
His lustrous bricks are brighter than blood,
His smoking mortar whiter than bone.

Set each sharp-edged, fire-bitten brick
Straight by the plumb-line's shivering length;
Make my marvellous wall so thick
Dead nor living may shake its strength.

Full as a crystal cup with drink
Is my cell with dreams, and quiet, and cool. . . .
Stop, old man! You must leave a chink;
How can I breathe? *You can't, you fool!*

Village Mystery

The woman in the pointed hood
And cloak blue-gray like a pigeon's wing,
Whose orchard climbs to the balsam-wood,
Has done a cruel thing.

To her back door-step came a ghost,
A girl who had been ten years dead,
She stood by the granite hitching-post
And begged for a piece of bread.

Now why should I, who walk alone,
Who am ironical and proud,
Turn, when a woman casts a stone
At a beggar in a shroud?

I saw the dead girl cringe and whine,
And cower in the weeping air—
But, oh, she was no kin of mine,
And so I did not care!

Escape

When foxes eat the last gold grape,
And the last white antelope is killed,
I shall stop fighting and escape
Into a little house I'll build.

But first I'll shrink to fairy size,
With a whisper no one understands,
Making blind moons of all your eyes,
And muddy roads of all your hands.

And you may grope for me in vain
In hollows under the mangrove root,
Or where, in apple-scented rain,
The silver wasp-nests hang like fruit.

"Fire and Sleet and Candlelight"

Poetry, April 1920

For this you've striven
  Daring to fail:
Your sky is riven
  Like a tearing veil.

For this, you've wasted
  Wings of your youth;
Divined, and tasted
  Bitter springs of truth.

From sand unslakèd
  Twisted strong cords,
And wandered naked
  Among trysted swords.

There's a word unspoken,
  A knot untied.
Whatever is broken
  The earth may hide.

The road was jagged
  Over sharp stones:
Your body's too ragged
  To cover your bones.

The wind scatters
  Tears upon dust;
Your soul's in tatters
  Where the spears thrust.

Your race is ended—
  See, it is run:
Nothing is mended
  Under the sun.

Straight as an arrow
    You fall to a sleep
Not too narrow
    And not too deep.

Sea Lullaby

The old moon is tarnished
With smoke of the flood,
The dead leaves are varnished
With colour like blood,

A treacherous smiler
With teeth white as milk,
A savage beguiler
In sheathings of silk,

The sea creeps to pillage,
She leaps on her prey;
A child of the village
Was murdered to-day.

She came up to meet him
In a smooth golden cloak,
She choked him and beat him
To death, for a joke.

Her bright locks were tangled,
She shouted for joy,
With one hand she strangled
A strong little boy.

Now in silence she lingers
Beside him all night
To wash her long fingers
In silvery light.

A Proud Lady

New York Evening Post, October 1920

Hate in the world's hand
Can carve and set its seal
Like the strong blast of sand
Which cuts into steel.

I have seen how the finger of hate
Can mar and mould
Faces burned passionate
And frozen cold.

Sorrowful faces worn
As stone with rain,
Faces writhing with scorn
And sullen with pain.

But you have a proud face
Which the world cannot harm,
You have turned the pain to a grace
And the scorn to a charm.

You have taken the arrows and slings
Which prick and bruise
And fashioned them into wings
For the heels of your shoes.

From the world's hand which tries
To tear you apart
You have stolen the falcon's eyes
And the lion's heart.

What has it done, this world,
With hard finger-tips,
But sweetly chiselled and curled
Your inscrutable lips?

Incantation

New York Evening Post, October 1920

A white well
In a black cave;
A bright shell
In a dark wave.

A white rose
Black brambles hood;
Smooth bright snows
In a dark wood.

A flung white glove
In a dark fight;
A white dove
On a wild black night.

A white door
In a dark lane;
A bright core
To bitter black pain.

A white hand
Waved from dark walls;
In a burnt black land
Bright waterfalls.

A bright spark
Where black ashes are;
In the smothering dark
One white star.

Silver Filigree

Poetry, April 1920

The icicles wreathing
On trees in festoon
Swing, swayed to our breathing:
They're made of the moon.

She's a pale, waxen taper;
And these seem to drip
Transparent as paper
From the flame of her tip.

Molten, smoking a little,
Into crystal they pass;
Falling, freezing, to brittle
And delicate glass.

Each a sharp-pointed flower,
Each a brief stalactite
Which hangs for an hour
In the blue cave of night.

The Falcon

Why should my sleepy heart be taught
To whistle mocking-bird replies?
This is another bird you've caught,
Soft-feathered, with a falcon's eyes.

The bird Imagination,
That flies so far, that dies so soon;
Her wings are coloured like the sun,
Her breast is coloured like the moon.

Weave her a chain of silver twist,
And a little hood of scarlet wool,
And let her perch upon your wrist,
And tell her she is beautiful.

Bronze Trumpets and Sea Water—On Turning Latin Into English

New Republic, April 1921

Alembics turn to stranger things
Strange things, but never while we live
Shall magic turn this bronze that sings
To singing water in a sieve.

The trumpeters of Cæsar's guard
Salute his rigorous bastions
With ordered bruit; the bronze is hard
Though there is silver in the bronze.

Our mutable tongue is like the sea,
Curled wave and shattering thunder-fit;
Dangle in strings of sand shall he
Who smooths the ripples out of it.

Spring Pastoral

Outlook, August 1920

Liza, go steep your long white hands
In the cool waters of that spring
Which bubbles up through shiny sands
The colour of a wild-dove's wing.

Dabble your hands, and steep them well
Until those nails are pearly white
Now rosier than a laurel bell;
Then come to me at candle light.

Lay your cold hands across my brows,
And I shall sleep, and I shall dream
Of silver-pointed willow boughs
Dipping their fingers in a stream.

Velvet Shoes

Poetry, April 1920

Let us walk in the white snow
In a soundless space;
With footsteps quiet and slow,
At a tranquil pace,
Under veils of white lace.

I shall go shod in silk,
And you in wool,
White as a white cow's milk,
More beautiful
Than the breast of a gull.

We shall walk through the still town
In a windless peace;
We shall step upon white down,
Upon silver fleece,
Upon softer than these.

We shall walk in velvet shoes:
Wherever we go
Silence will fall like dews
On white silence below.
We shall walk in the snow.

Valentine

New Republic, January 1921

Too high, too high to pluck
My heart shall swing.
A fruit no bee shall suck,
No wasp shall sting.

If on some night of cold
It falls to ground
In apple-leaves of gold
I'll wrap it round.

And I shall seal it up
With spice and salt,
In a carven silver cup,
In a deep vault.

Before my eyes are blind
And my lips mute,
I must eat core and rind
Of that same fruit.

Before my heart is dust
At the end of all,
Eat it I must, I must
Were it bitter gall.

But I shall keep it sweet
By some strange art;
Wild honey I shall eat
When I eat my heart.

O honey cool and chaste
As clover's breath!
Sweet Heaven I shall taste
Before my death.

CHAPTER THREE

From *Black Armour*

New York: George Doran Company, 1923
London: Martin Secker, 1928
Collected Poems of Elinor Wylie. New York: Alfred A. Knopf, 1932

Full Moon

New Republic, June 1922
Current Opinion, August 1923

My bands of silk and miniver
Momently grew heavier;
The black gauze was beggarly thin;
The ermine muffled mouth and chin;
I could not suck the moonlight in.

Harlequin in lozenges
Of love and hate, I walked in these
Striped and ragged rigmaroles;
Along the pavement my footsoles
Trod warily on living coals.

Shouldering the thoughts I loathed,
In their corrupt disguises clothed,
Mortality I could not tear
From my ribs, to leave them bare
Ivory in silver air.

There I walked, and there I raged;
The spiritual savage caged
Within my skeleton, raged afresh
To feel, behind a carnal mesh,
The clean bones crying in the flesh.

Nebuchadnezzar

New Republic, December 1921

My body is weary to death of my mischievous brain;
I am weary forever and ever of being brave;
Therefore I crouch on my knees while the cool white rain
Curves the clover over my head like a wave.

The stem and the frosty seed of the grass are ripe;
I have devoured their strength; I have drunk them deep;
And the dandelion is gall in a thin green pipe,
But the clover is honey and sun and the smell of sleep.

Prophecy

Century, February 1922

I shall lie hidden in a hut
  In the middle of an alder wood,
With the back door blind and bolted shut,
  And the front door locked for good.

I shall lie folded like a saint,
  Lapped in a scented linen sheet,
On a bedstead striped with bright-blue paint,
  Narrow and cold and neat.

The midnight will be glassy black
  Behind the panes, with wind about
To set his mouth against a crack
  And blow the candle out.

Epitaph

New Republic, May 1922

For this she starred her eyes with salt
And scooped her temples thin,
Until her face shone pure of fault
From the forehead to the chin.

In coldest crucibles of pain
Her shrinking flesh was fired
And smoothed into a finer grain
To make it more desired.

Pain left her lips more clear than glass;
It coloured and cooled her hand.
She lay a field of scented grass
Yielded as pasture land.

For this her loveliness was curved
And carved as silver is:
For this she was brave; but she deserved
A better grave than this.

Song

New Republic, June 1927

It is my thoughts that colour
My soul which slips between;
Thoughts lunar and solar
And gold and sea-green

Tint the pure translucence
Of the crystal thread;
A rainbow nuisance
It runs through my head.

When I am dead, or sleeping
Without any pain,
My soul will stop creeping
Through my jewelled brain.

With no brightness to dye it
None will see where
It flows clear and quiet
As a river of air;

Watering dark places
Without sparkle or sound;
Kissing dumb faces
And the dusty ground.

Heroics

New Republic, June 1922
Bookman, September 1922

Though here and there a man is left
Whose iron thread eludes the shears,
The martyr with his bosom cleft
Is dead these seven heavy years.

Does he survive whose tongue was slit,
To slake some envy of a king's?
Sportive silver cried from it
Before the savage cut the strings.

The rack has crumpled up the limb
Stretched immediate to fly;
Never ask the end of him
Stubborn to outstare the sky.

Assuming an heroic mask,
He stands a tall derisive tree,
While servile to the speckled task
We move devoted hand and knee.

It is no virtue, but a fault
Thus to breathe ignoble air,
Suffering unclean assault
And insult dubious to bear.

Preference

Measure: A Journal of Poetry, July 1922

These to me are beautiful people;
Thick hair sliding in a ripple;
A tall throat, round as a column;
A mournful mouth, small and solemn,
Having to confound the mourner
Irony in either corner;
The limbs fine, narrow and strong;
Like the wind they walk along,
Like the whirlwind, bad to follow;
The cheekbones high, the cheeks hollow,
The eyes large and wide apart.
They carry a dagger in the heart
So keen and clean it never rankles. . . .
They wear small bones in wrists and ankles.

Let No Charitable Hope

Literary Digest, July 1922
Current Opinion, August 1923

Now let no charitable hope
Confuse my mind with images
Of eagle and of antelope:
I am in nature none of these.

I was, being human, born alone;
I am, being woman, hard beset;
I live by squeezing from a stone
The little nourishment I get.

In masks outrageous and austere
The years go by in single file;
But none has merited my fear,
And none has quite escaped my smile.

Self-portrait

New Republic, March 1922

A lens of crystal whose transparence calms
Queer stars to clarity, and disentangles
Fox-fires to form austere refracted angles:
A texture polished on the horny palms
Of vast equivocal creatures, beast or human:
A flint, a substance finer-grained than snow,
Graved with the Graces in intaglio
To set sarcastic sigil on the woman.

This for the mind, and for the little rest
A hollow scooped to blackness in the breast,
The simulacrum of a cloud, a feather:
Instead of stone, instead of sculptured strength,
The soul, this vanity, blown hither and thither
By trivial breath, over the whole world's length.

Cold-blooded Creatures

New Republic, August 1921

Man, the egregious egoist
(In mystery the twig is bent),
Imagines, by some mental twist,
That he alone is sentient

Of the intolerable load
Which on all living creatures lies,
Nor stoops to pity in the toad
The speechless sorrow of its eyes.

He asks no questions of the snake,
Nor plumbs the phosphorescent gloom
Where lidless fishes, broad awake,
Swim staring at a night-mare doom.

King Honour's Eldest Son

Vanity Fair, April 1923

His father's steel, piercing the wholesome fruit
Of his mother's flesh, wrought acidly to mar
Its own Damascus, staining worse than war
A purity intense and absolute;
While her clean stock put forth a poisoned shoot,
In likeness of a twisted scimitar,
Sleek as a lovelock, ugly as a scar,
Wrong as the firstborn of a mandrake root.

There was a waning moon upon his brow,
A fallen star upon his pointed chin;
He mingled Ariel with Caliban;
But such a blossom upon such a bough
Convinced his poor progenitors of sin
In having made a something more than man.

Nonchalance

New Republic, August 1921

This cool and laughing mind, renewed
From covert sources like a spring's,
Is potent to translate the mood
Of all distraught and twisted things.

In this clear water shall be cast
Outrageous shapes of steel and gold,
And all their hot and clotted past
Beaded with bubbles silver-cold.

The moving power takes their heat
Into itself, forgetting them;
And warmth in trickles, slow and sweet
Comforts a fainting lily-stem.

Demon Lovers

New Republic, June 1922

The peacock and the mocking-bird
Cry forever in her breast;
Public libraries have blurred
The pages of his palimpsest.

He wanders lonely as a cloud
In chevelure of curled perruque;
Masked assassins in a crowd
Strangle the uxorious duke.

Castilian facing Lucifer,
Juan does not remove his cap;
Unswadddled infantile to her
His soul lies kicking in her lap.

While she, transported by the wind,
Mercutio has clasped and kissed. . . .
Like quicksilver, her absent mind
Evades them both, and is not missed.

Castilian

New Republic, November 1921

Velasquez took a pliant knife
And scraped his palette clean;
He said, "I lead a dog's own life
Painting a king and queen."

He cleaned his palette with oily rags
And oakum from Seville wharves;
"I am sick of painting painted hags
And bad ambiguous dwarves.

"The sky is silver, the clouds are pearl,
Their locks are looped with rain.
I will not paint Maria's girl
For all the money in Spain."

He washed his face in water cold,
His hands in turpentine;
He squeezed out colour like coins of gold
And colour like drops of wine.

Each colour lay like a little pool
On the polished cedar wood;
Clear and pale and ivory-cool
Or dark as solitude.

He burnt the rags in the fireplace
And leaned from the window high;
He said, "I like that gentleman's face
Who wears his cap awry."

This is the gentleman, there he stands,
Castilian, sombre-caped,
With arrogant eyes, and narrow hands
Miraculously shaped.

Sequence

Vanity Fair, November 1922

I
This is the end of all, and yet I strive
To fight for nothing, having nothing kept
Of loveliness that saved myself alive
Before this killing distillation crept
Numbing my limbs, and stiffening my tongue
To clay, less vital than the salted thorn
Whereon a tyrant's banneret is hung
As scarecrow for a harvesting still-born:
And I am barren in a barren land,
But who so breaks me, I shall pierce his hand.

This much is true, that there were certain times,
Measured by minutes, with a blank between,
When our two courages could meet, and climb
Into the blue above the blowing green;
But now the lifted pasture is too high,
The shoal too deep, for such were noble graves;
In this unlighted kennel, where to die
Will not awaken hounds, nor anger slaves,
I shall advise me to prepare my couch;
Here it is dark, for more I may not vouch.

II
One of these men will find my skeleton;
To one it will be delicate and slim,
With stars for eyes, and portent of a sun
Rising between the ribs to frighten him;
Yet, being bold, he might embrace it soon
With quick insensate passion in the night,
And by the holy taper of the moon
Encouraged, and because its bones were light
As filagree of pearl, he might depart
Bearing my jangled heart-strings on his heart.

And he might bury it in sand or sod,
Stamping it down to circumvent the wolf,
And, being kind, commend it to his God,
Whose Mind was swimming somewhere in the gulf
Above his head; but if that other found
The rotten framework of his servitor,
He'd leave it lying on the cluttered ground
Between a bottle and an apple-core,
And go his way, in agony and sweat,
Because he could not pity nor forget.

III

For various questions which I shall not ask,
And various answers which I cannot hear,
I have contrived a substituted task
To prove my body is devoid of fear;
To prove my spirit's elemental blood
Is pure, courageous, and uniform,
I shall submerge my body in the mud,
I shall submit my spirit to the storm;
I shall bend down my bosom to the snake,
As to an infant for its father's sake.

I shall persist, I shall pursue my way
Believing that his cruelty was fine
As tempered steel for chastening of clay,
Impatient of corrosions that were mine;
He that despised me shall not be forgot;
He that disparaged me shall be my lord;
That was a flambeau, half-consumed and hot,
This was the running light along a sword;
And though I warmed my fingers at the one,
The other is my father and my son.

Benvenuto's Valentine

Yale Review, April 1923

Not for the child that wanders home
So wasted by barbaric kings,
So wearied by imperial Rome
That he will clasp my apron-strings.

Not for the ghost that never is
And never will be known by me,
Whose heel is on the precipice
Before its print has left the sea.

And not for darling Harlequin
Spinning in stars of diamond shape;
Nor Hamlet exquisite and thin
As moonbeams in an inky cape.

Not for the legend latest-born
Of Chivalry and Virgin, whom
Roland has knighted with a horn,
And Richard with a sprig of broom.

Not even for the man who climbed
A thousand miles to thrust a torch
Among forgotten fagots, rimed
By winter in an iron porch.

But for the thought, that wrought and planned
Such intricate and crystal things,
My kiss is set upon your hand
As softly as a silver ring's.

Twelfth Night

Literary Digest, December 1922
Yale Review, January 1923

It has always been King Herod that I feared;
King Herod and his kinsmen, ever since. . . .
I do not like the colour of your beard;
I think that you are wicked, and a prince.

I keep no stable . . . how your horses stamp! . . .
If you are wise men, you will leave me soon;
I have been frightened by a thievish tramp
Who counted bloody silver in the moon.

You get no lodging underneath these roofs,
No, though you pay in frankincense and myrrh;
Your harness jangles with your horses' hooves;
Be quiet; you will wake him if you stir.

This is no church for Zoroastrians,
Nor resting-place for governors from Rome;
Oh, I have knowledge of your secret plans;
Your faces are familiar; go home.

And you, young captain of the lion stare,
Subdue your arrogance to this advice;
You should forbid your soldiery to swear,
To spit at felons, and to play at dice.

You have perceived, above the chimney ledge,
Hanging inverted by Saint David's harp,
His sword from heaven, with the double edge
Which, for your service, is no longer sharp.

He sleeps, like some ingenuous shepherd boy
Or carpenter's apprentice, but his slim
And wounded hands shall never more destroy
Another giant; do not waken him.

The counterpane conceals the deeper wound
    Which lately I have washed with vinegar;
Now let this iron bar be importuned;
    I say you shall not speak to him of war.

Now That Your Eyes Are Shut

Outlook, June 1922
Current Opinion, August 1923

Now that your eyes are shut
Not even a dusty butterfly may brush them;
My flickering knife has cut
Life from sonorous lion throats to hush them.

If pigeons croon too loud
Or lambs bleat proudly, they must come to slaughter,
And I command each cloud
To be precise in spilling silent water.

Let light forbear those lids;
I have forbidden the feathery ash to smutch them;
The spider thread that thrids
The gray-plumed grass has not my leave to touch them.

My casual ghost may slip,
Issuing tiptoe, from the pure inhuman;
The tissues of my lip
Will bruise your eyelids, while I am a woman.

Parting Gift

Outlook, June 1922
Current Opinion, August 1923

I cannot give you the Metropolitan Tower;
I cannot give you heaven;
Nor the nine Visigoth crowns in the Cluny Museum;
Nor happiness, even.
But I can give you a very small purse
Made out of field-mouse skin,
With a painted picture of the universe
And seven blue tears therein.

I cannot give you the island of Capri;
I cannot give you beauty;
Nor bake you marvellous crusty cherry pies
With love and duty.
But I can give you a very little locket
Made out of wildcat hide:
Put it into your left-hand pocket
And never look inside.

On a Singing Girl

Literary Digest, December 1926

Musa of the sea-blue eyes,
Silver nightingale, alone
In a little coffin lies:
A stone beneath a stone.

She, whose song we loved the best,
Is voiceless in a sudden night:
On your light limbs, O loveliest,
May the dust be light!

To Claudia Homonœa

My words were delicately breathed
As Syren notes: the Cyprian's head
Never shone out more golden-wreathed
Than mine: but now I lie here dead.

A chattering swallow, bright and wild,
Whom one man loved for all her years—
Having loved her even as a child:
I leave him nothing but his tears.

CHAPTER FOUR

From *Trivial Breath*

New York: Alfred Knopf, 1928
Collected Poems of Elinor Wylie. New York: Alfred A. Knopf, 1932

Dedication

New Republic, November 1927

When I was seven years old I had a primer:
The immaculate bosom of the mother-tongue
Flowed milkily in mercy to the young,
Dispensing balsam to the infant dreamer.
How delicately did the silver skimmer
Of natural love select the cream along
The honied surface of that stream of song!
That cup of pearls dissolving into dimmer!

That breast of twin benevolent moons! That conduit
Whose veins are threaded with pellucid truth!
Into the hungry coffin and beyond it
A single uncorrupted drop of youth
Must live in elegy upon my lips
When I and chaos shall have come to grips.

I would that my possessions were the proper
And polished coinage of the stars and suns;
But for the earth I give you farthing bronze,
And for the planets I return you copper.
Fumes fallen from your ceremonial supper
Made aromatic harmony which once
Refreshed my childhood: even now it runs
Between our skies, the lower and the upper.

Oh, who was I to be so bravely suckled
At the early wells of English undefiled,
And by your grace, whose sacred hand unbuckled
Extreme Castalia for a careless child?
Yet this I grant the creature of uncommon;
She is your vassal while she is a woman.

That creature is your vassal ever since:
Perceiving the device upon your standard
To be the sign her infancy had pondered,
Her spirit was impulsive to convince.

If her opinion perishes or wins;
Be her fidelity approved or slandered;
The event is set: the woman never wandered
In vile devotion to a lesser prince.

Profuse and fabulous appeared the page
On which your youngest lessons were emblazoned:
Enchantments that unlock a crystal cage;
An alphabet with astral fire seasoned;
These are the characters of that largesse
Which gives the lavish greater to the less.

For that her blood is valiant and noble
I thank the language at her leaping source;
At best essential heaven; at bitter worse
A witch's brew of strong fantastic trouble:
But for your courtesy my thanks are double,
Who, as a matter of munificent course,
Diverted waves of influential force
To shape for me a rainbow-coloured bubble.

An innocent bird, an iridescent music,
To be my own for all the rest of living.
Oh, this was nourishment and wine and physic!
This was a proud extravagance of giving!
And I have nothing to return in kind
Save the dull mortal homage of the mind.

"Desolation Is a Delicate Thing"

New Republic, January 1928

Sorrow lay upon my breast more heavily than winter clay
Lying ponderable upon the unmoving bosom of the dead;
Yet it was dissolved like a thin snowfall; it was softly withered away;
Presently like a single drop of dew it had trembled and fled.

This sorrow, which seemed heavier than a shovelful of loam,
Was gone like water, like a web of delicate frost;
It was silent and vanishing like smoke; it was scattered like foam;
Though my mind should desire to preserve it, nevertheless it is lost.

This sorrow was not like sorrow; it was shining and brief;
Even as I waked and was aware of its going, it was past and gone;
It was not earth; it was no more than a light leaf,
Or a snowflake in spring, which perishes upon stone.

This sorrow was small and vulnerable and short-lived;
It was neither earth nor stone; it was silver snow
Fallen from heaven, perhaps; it has not survived
An hour of the sun; it is sad it should be so.

This sorrow, which I believed a gravestone over my heart,
Is gone like a cloud; it eluded me as I woke;
Its crystal dust is suddenly broken and blown apart;
It was not my heart; it was this poor sorrow alone which broke.

Minotaur

New Republic, June 1923

Go study to disdain
The frail, the over-fine
Which tapers to a line
Knotted about the brain.

Unscrupulous to pinch
And polish down the thin
And fire-encasing skin:
Which pares away an inch

Of valuable soil
Whereon a god took root,
Diminishing a brute
With pumice and with oil.

Distrust the exquisite,
The sharpened silver nerve,
The lacquered, nacred curve
Wherein a moon is lit.

Aristocratic skulls
Rejected as inept
That innocency kept
'Twixt orbèd eyes of bulls.

Black lava-crusted coins
Bear heavy brow and limb,
The monstrous stamp of him
Who sprang from Taurine loins.

Gaze ever and at length
Upon the carven head,
Devouring it as bread
To thrive upon its strength.

The sword-deflecting scar
Indented and oblique
That stripes the savage cheek;
The throat made columnar

In copper, and up-raised
To such a trumpet shape
No clangour can escape,—
These only must be praised.

This only is the cure,
To clasp the creature fast;
The flesh survives at last
Because it is not pure.

From flesh refined to glass
A god goes desert-ward,
Astride a spotted pard,
Between an ox and ass.

Let innocence enchant
The flesh to fiercer grain
More fitted to retain
This burning visitant.

Confession of Faith

New Republic, February 1924

I lack the braver mind
That dares to find
The lover friend, and kind.

I fear him to the bone;
I lie alone
By the beloved one,

And, breathless for suspense,
Erect defense
Against love's violence

Whose silences portend
A bloody end
For lover never friend.

But, in default of faith,
In futile breath,
I dream no ill of Death.

True Vine

New Republic, April 1927

There is a serpent in perfection tarnished,
The thin shell pierced, the purity grown fainter,
The virgin silver shield no longer burnished,
The pearly fruit with ruin for its centre.

The thing that sits expectant in our bosoms
Contriving heaven out of very little
Demands such delicate immaculate blossoms
As no malicious verity makes brittle.

The wild fastidious hope is quick to languish;
Its smooth diaphanous escape is swifter
Than the pack of truth; no mortal can distinguish
Its trace upon the durable hereafter.

Not so the obdurate and savage lovely
Whose roots are set profoundly upon trouble;
This flower grows so fiercely and so bravely
It does not even know that it is noble.

This is the vine to love, whose balsams flourish
Upon a living soil corrupt and faulty,
Whose leaves have drunk the skies, and stooped to nourish
The earth again with honey sweet and salty.

Speed the Parting——

I shall not sprinkle with dust
A creature so clearly lunar;
You must die—but of course you must—
And better later than sooner.
But if it should be in a year
That year itself must perish;
How dingy a thing is fear,
And sorrow, how dull to cherish!
And if it should be in a day
That day would be dark by evening,
But the morning might still be gay
And the moon have golden leavening.
And beauty's a moonlight grist
That comes to the mills of dying;
The silver grain may be missed
But there's no great good in crying.
Though luminous things are mould
They survive in a glance that crossed them,
And it's not very kind to scold
The empty air that has lost them.
The limpid blossom of youth
Turns into a poison berry;
Having perceived this truth
I shall not weep but be merry.
Therefore die when you please;
It's not very wise to worry;
I shall not shiver and freeze;
I shall not even be sorry.
Beautiful things are wild;
They are gone, and you go after;
Therefore I mean, my child,
To charm your going with laughter.
Love and pity are strong,
But wisdom is happily greater;
You will die, I suppose, before long.
Oh, worser sooner than later!

Hospes Comesque Corporis

New Republic, January 1928

And if the heart may split the skin
Of this intrinsic chrysalis
To make the ephemeral ghost within
The fugitive it is:

If even the thinnest ravelling bind
Escape to the abandoned shell:
The heart must set the hollow mind
Replying like a bell.

Before division of the suns
Take shears to cut a second's thread,
The mind must tick ecstatic once
To prove that it is dead.

And the small soul's dissolving ghost
Must leave a heart-shape in the dust
Before it is inspired and lost
In God: I hope it must.

Peter and John

New Republic, April 1924

Twelve good friends
Walked under the leaves,
Binding the ends
Of the barley sheaves.

Peter and John
Lay down to sleep
Pillowed upon
A haymaker's heap.

John and Peter
Lay down to dream.
The air was sweeter
Than honey and cream.

Peter was bred
In the salty cold:
His hair was red
And his eyes were gold.

John had a mouth
Like a wing bent down:
His brow was smooth
And his eyes were brown.

Peter to slumber
Sank like a stone,
Of all their number
The bravest one.

John more slowly
Composed himself,
Young and holy
Among the Twelve.

John as he slept
Cried out in grief,
Turned and wept
On the golden leaf:

"Peter, Peter,
Stretch me your hand
Across the glitter
Of the harvest land!

"Peter, Peter,
Give me a sign!
This was a bitter
Dream of mine—

"Bitter as aloes
It parched my tongue.
Upon the gallows
My life was hung.

"Sharp it seemed
As a bloody sword.
Peter, I dreamed
I was Christ the Lord!"

Peter turned
To holy Saint John:
His body burned
In the falling sun.

In the falling sun
He burned like flame:
"John, Saint John,
I have dreamed the same!

"My bones were hung
On an elder tree;

Bells were rung
Over Galilee.

"A silver penny
Sealed each of my eyes.
Many and many
A cock crew thrice."

When Peter's word
Was spoken and done,
"Were you Christ the Lord
In your dream?" said John.

"No," said the other,
"That I was not.
I was our brother
Iscariot."

A Strange Story

New Republic, April 1924

When I died in Berners Street
I remember well
That I had lights at head and feet
And a passing bell.

But when I died in Houndsditch
There came to lay me out
A washerwoman and a witch;
The rats ran about.

When I died in Holborn
In an old house and tall
I know the tapestry was torn
And hanging from the wall.

When I died in Marylebone
I was saying my prayers;
There I died all alone
Up four flights of stairs.

But when I died near Lincoln's Inn
The small gold I had
Surrounded me with kith and kin;
I died stark mad.

When I died in Bloomsbury
In the bend of your arm,
At the end I died merry
And comforted and warm.

The Puritan's Ballad

Bookman, April 1923

My love came up from Barnegat,
  The sea was in his eyes;
He trod as softly as a cat
  And told me terrible lies.

His hair was yellow as new-cut pine
  In shavings curled and feathered;
I thought how silver it would shine
  By cruel winters weathered.

But he was in his twentieth year,
  This time I'm speaking of;
We were head over heels in love with fear
  And half a-feared of love.

His feet were used to treading a gale
  And balancing thereon;
His face was brown as a foreign sail
  Threadbare against the sun.

His arms were thick as hickory logs
  Whittled to little wrists;
Strong as the teeth of terrier dogs
  Were the fingers of his fists.

Within his arms I feared to sink
  Where lions shook their manes,
And dragons drawn in azure ink
  Leapt quickened by his veins.

Dreadful his strength and length of limb
  As the sea to foundering ships;
I dipped my hands in love for him
  No deeper than their tips.

But our palms were welded by a flame
  The moment we came to part,
And on his knuckles I read my name
  Enscrolled within a heart.

And something made our wills to bend
  As wild as trees blown over;
We were no longer friend and friend,
  But only lover and lover.

"In seven weeks or seventy years—
  God grant it may be sooner!—
I'll make a handkerchief for your tears
  From the sails of my captain's schooner.

"We'll wear our loves like wedding rings
  Long polished to our touch;
We shall be busy with other things
  And they cannot bother us much.

"When you are skimming the wrinkled cream
  And your ring clinks on the pan,
You'll say to yourself in a pensive dream,
  'How wonderful a man!'

"When I am slitting a fish's head
  And my ring clanks on the knife,
I'll say with thanks, as a prayer is said,
  'How beautiful a wife!'

"And I shall fold my decorous paws
  In velvet smooth and deep,
Like a kitten that covers up its claws
  To sleep and sleep and sleep.

"Like a little blue pigeon you shall bow
  Your bright alarming crest;

In the crook of my arm you'll lay your brow
  To rest and rest and rest."

Will he never come back from Barnegat
  With thunder in his eyes,
Treading as soft as a tiger cat,
  To tell me terrible lies?

The Devil in Seven Shires
A Carol for Midsummer Eve

Come all ye sorrowful people
Who would escape my fires;
Climb to the top of the steeple
And I'll show you seven shires.

The first is the shire of rivers;
The shire of a double dream
Whose image never shivers
In its mercurial stream.

The towers of Ys have hollowed
Tall caverns in the waves,
So this smooth stream has swallowed
A hundred hermits' caves,

A hundred wells of peace, no less,
And not a single town;
This is the shire for weariness;
Dive into this, and drown.

The second is the shire of iron
Where swords grow up like grain,
And granite walls environ
A broad resounding plain.

This radiant plain amazes
All men of noble will,
Where daggers grow like daisies;
Leap into this, and kill.

The third is the shire of apples
That are sweeter than holy bread;
I have torn down all the chapels
And builded inns instead;

Cider and beer in barrels;
And no man needs to think

Of war or money or quarrels;
Drop into this, and drink.

The fourth is the shire of sovereigns;
They cover the ground like leaves.
Thank God no justice governs
This heaven of my thieves!

They say the gold was given in alms
For Jesus Christ His sake,
But if any of you have itching palms
Steal into this, and take.

The fifth is the shire of whispers;
Its willow trees have tongues,
And soft infernal vespers
Ring bells between their songs;

And if you would betray your lord
Or see your brother die,
It needs, perhaps, but half a word;
Creep into this, and lie.

The sixth is the shire of shadows;
It shines within a cloud;
Silver are all its meadows;
Its birds sing low and loud;

Its clover valleys lie asleep
Forgetting to be sad;
If you would bury sorrow deep,
Go seek it, and go mad.

The seventh is the shire of pigeons
Queen Venus calls her doves,
Of Puck's and Pan's religions
And Ashtaroth her groves.

Ho! Young man with the missal-book,
What are you dreaming of?
Look in the bower below you, look!
Lean into this, and love.

“As I Went Down by Havre de Grace . . .”

New Republic, April 1928

As I went down by Havre de Grace
I saw the laurel in the wood:
The hours (I said) are sands that pass,
And some are bad and some are good;
Some are black and some are bright,
Yet all were darker, I suppose,
In lands where laurel is waxen white
And never white suffused with rose.

As I went up by Forty Fort
I saw the dogwood on the hills:
Life (I said) is hard and short
And riddled by a hundred ills:
Yet how much heavier I had gone,
How far from all my heart’s desire,
In lands where dogwood never shone
Twisted by a tongue of fire.

As I went on by Steepletop
I saw wild strawberries underfoot:
Life (I said) is a water-drop
That falls upon a rotten root:
Yet were my grave the more profound
And planted thick with worser seeds,
Had I been nourished in a ground
Where strawberries never grow wild like weeds.

As I looked over by Isle au Haut
I saw the balsam in the grove:
Life (I said) is a flake of snow
That melts upon the bough above:
And I am murdered and undone,
But I was not bred in the middle land
Or in any valley under the sun
Where these dark trees disdain to stand.

As I went out by Prettymarsh
I saw the mayflower under the leaves:
Life (I said) is rough and harsh
And fretted by a hundred griefs:
Yet were it more than I could face,
Who have faced out a hundred dooms,
Had I been born in any place
Where this small flower never blooms.

False Prophet

When I was forty, and two feathers sprung
Like crescents silver-curved from either temple,
Above a casque of bronze, I saw the simple
And casual shape of beauty; and my tongue
Spoke thus: "I am rejoiced I am not young
Lest this supreme and ultimate example
Of fine-spun flesh should very lightly trample
Upon my wounds; my withers are unwrung."

He might have been my son, save that my youth,
Bending the slender bow of its despair,
Loosed no such luminous arrow on the air;
His shaft was cut from some diviner bough:
And while my fainting heart perceived the truth,
My tongue spoke thus: "He cannot hurt me now."

A Red Carpet for Shelley

New Republic, January 1927

I

But this is nothing; an eccentric joke,
The legendary patchwork of a year
Flung into muddiness, like Raleigh's cloak,
To ask the honour of your step, my dear.
Your path is printed on the atmosphere
Forever as a flame against the smoke
Of obscure vision, and I must invoke
Your magnanimity to make it clear.

If I might spread soft words like living grass
Laid smooth beneath the heavy wheels of Time;
If I might loose the river of a rhyme
Or build a pavement out of gold and glass
Providing Heaven for you to walk upon,
It would be well; it would be better done.

II

The only engine which can fabricate
Language from spirit is the heart of each;
Industrious blood has braided into speech
The airy filaments of love and hate.
I have the labour of my own estate,
A pitiful machine which shall not reach
A single stellar thread; I cannot teach
Its narrow nerves the virtue to be great.

If my devout affection had been given
Commensurate power, which doubt nor custom dulls;
If I possessed the pure and fiery pulse
By true divinity informed and driven,
I would unroll the rounded moon and sun
And knit them up for you to walk upon.

III

The little sum of my experience
Remains the sole contrivance I produce
To weave this mesh, to colour and confuse
These ragged syllables with soul and sense.
I have been put to one supreme expense;
This was the noblest tincture I could use,
This the most subtle grain; I cannot choose
The dye to turn the lacklustre intense.

I have the proper scarlet of my veins,
The clean involved precision of my mind,
And you, who are so excellently kind,
Will not reject the tissue of my pains,
Stained by mortality's vermilion
To make a world for you to walk upon.

IV

Forgive the savage texture of the spoil
Tinted so barbarously by the clay
The rusty iron and the ocean-spray
Which lifted up my body from the soil.
Forgive the complicated brittle coil
Of my infirm invention, which I lay
Where you may pause, and pass, and never stay.
Here are the shocks of maize, the honey and oil,

The fruits like harvest moons, the fabulous land,
The crystal hills, the veiled prismatic plain;
And you will come, and you will not remain,
Nor leave a trace along the gilded sand.
So presently you will be come and gone;
Here's a strange road for you to walk upon.

Address to My Soul

Poetry, May 1928

My soul, be not disturbed
By planetary war;
Remain securely orbed
In this contracted star.

Fear not, pathetic flame;
Your sustenance is doubt:
Glassed in translucent dream
They cannot snuff you out.

Wear water, or a mask
Of unapparent cloud;
Be brave and never ask
A more defunctive shroud.

The universal points
Are shrunk into a flower;
Between its delicate joints
Chaos keeps no power.

The pure integral form,
Austere and silver-dark,
Is balanced on the storm
In its predestined arc.

Small as a sphere of rain
It slides along the groove
Whose path is furrowed plain
Among the suns that move.

The shapes of April buds
Outlive the phantom year:
Upon the void at odds
The dewdrop falls severe.

Five-petalled flame, be cold:
Be firm, dissolving star:
Accept the stricter mould
That makes you singular.

Last Supper

Poetry, November 1928

Now that the shutter of the dusk
  Begins to tremble in its groove,
I am constrained to strip the husk
  From everything I truly love.

So short a time remains to taste
  The ivory pulp, the seven pips,
My heart is happy without haste
  With revelation at its lips.

So calm a beauty shapes the core,
  So grave a blossom frames the stem,
In this last minute and no more
  My eyes alone shall eat of them.

Lament for Glasgerion

Poetry, June and November 1928

The lovely body of the dead,
Wherein he laid him down to rest,
Is shrunken to corruption's thread;
The blood which delicately dressed
The flying bone, the sighing breast,
One with nothingness is made.

The darling garment is outworn;
Its fabric nourishes the moth;
The silk wherein his soul was born,
Woven of flesh and spirit both,
Is crumpled to a pitiful cloth:
His soul lies naked and forlorn.

So one that walks within the air,
Who loves the ghost below the ground,
Rejoices fervently to wear
A body shaken and unsound;
A brow divided by a wound;
A throat encircled by a care.

Shall I go warm above the cold
Wherein he sleeps without a shroud
Or shred of beauty left to fold
About the poor soul's solitude?
The vanishing dust of my heart is proud
To watch me wither and grow old.

Tragic Dialogue

New Republic, March 1928

"Does not the progressive wheel of years
Composed of baser metals
Obscure him from your eyes, whose tears
Have turned to willow petals?

"A hundred years! This iron bar
Has beaten you, and hindered?"
"Not so: on no extremest star
Had he and I been kindred.

"Ah no, both happily and alas!
A clover field, a river,
A hawthorn hedge, a pane of glass
Had parted us forever."

CHAPTER FIVE

From *Angels and Earthly Creatures*

New York and London: Alfred A. Knopf, 1929
Collected Poems of Elinor Wylie. New York: Alfred A. Knopf, 1932

One Person

Henley-on-Thames: Borough Press, 1928
New Republic, January 1929

Although these words are false, none shall prevail
To prove them in translation less than true
Or overthrow their dignity, or undo
The faith implicit in a fabulous tale;
The ashes of this error shall exhale
Essential verity, and two by two
Lovers devout and loyal shall renew
The legend, and refuse to let it fail.

Even the betrayer and the fond deceived,
Having put off the body of this death,
Shall testify with one remaining breath,
From sepulchres demand to be believed:
These words are true, although at intervals
The unfaithful clay contrive to make them false.

I

Now shall the long homesickness have an end
Upon your heart, which is a part of all
The past no human creature may recall
Save you, who are persuasive to unbend
The brows of death, and name him for a friend:
This ecstasy is supernatural;
I have survived to see the heavens fall
Into my hands, which on your hands depend.

Time has prepared us an enduring bed
Within the earth of this beloved land;
And, lying side by side and hand in hand,
We sleep coeval with the happy dead
Who are ourselves, a little earlier bound
To one another's bosom in the ground.

II

What other name had half expressed the whole
Of that incomparable and touching grace
Which spells the shape of danger in your face?
It is the very pattern of your soul;
The eagle's home, above the moon's control,
Above the seas, the high precipitate place;
The stairway cut from planetary space;
The crystal steps which climb a steeper goal.

The shadow of its light is only this:
That all your beauty is the work of wars
Between the upper and the nether stars;
Its symmetry is perfect and severe
Because the barbarous force of agonies
Broke it, and mended it, and made it clear.

III

"Children and dogs are subject to my power,"
You said, and smiled, and I beside you smiled,
Perceiving my unwisdom of a child,
My courage of a wolf new-taught to cower:
Upon the grass, beneath the falling flower,
I saw my spirit silent and beguiled
Standing at gaze; a brute no longer wild;
An infant wearied by the difficult hour.

And am I not your child who has come home?
And am I not your hound for faithfulness?
Put forth your hand, put forth your hand to bless
A creature stricken timorous and dumb,
Who now regards you with a lover's eyes
And knows that you are merciful and wise.

IV

Now am I Orson to your Valentine
Forever, and I choose it shall be so;

For how should the uncivil brier grow
Germane in nature to the noble vine?
The savage should be servant to the fine;
The falcon fly superior to the crow;
O dear my lord, believe me that I know
How far your virtues have outnumbered mine.

And you have levied final tribute now—
Your chivalry demanding the pretence—
You have constrained your vassal to avow
That we are equals, lest a violence
Be suffered by our love, and so I must
Deny the intrinsic difference in our dust.

V

The little beauty that I was allowed—
The lips new-cut and coloured by my sire,
The polished hair, the eyes' perceptive fire—
Has never been enough to make me proud:
For I have moved companioned by a cloud,
And lived indifferent to the blood's desire
Of temporal loveliness in vain attire:
My flesh was but a fresh-embroidered shroud.

Now do I grow indignant at the fate
Which made me so imperfect to compare
With your degree of noble and of fair;
Our elements are the farthest skies apart;
And I enjoin you, ere it is too late,
To stamp your superscription on my heart.

VI

I have believed that I prefer to live
Preoccupied by a Platonic mind;
I have believed me obdurate and blind
To those sharp ecstasies the pulses give:
The clever body five times sensitive

I never have discovered to be kind
As the poor soul, deceived and half-divined,
Whose hopes are water in a witch's sieve.

O now both soul and body are unfit
To apprehend this miracle, my lord!
Not all my senses, striving in accord
With my pure essence, are aware of it
Save as a power remote and exquisite,
Not seen or known, but fervently adored.

VII

Would I might make subliminal my flesh
And so contrive a gentle atmosphere
To comfort you because I am not there;
Or else incorporate and carve afresh
A lady, from the chilly heaven and clear
Which flows around you like a stream of air,
To warm and wind you in her body's mesh.

So would I cherish you a loving twice;
Once in a mist made matter; once again
In my true substance made ethereal:
And yet I cannot succour you at all
Whose letter cries, "My hands are cold as ice,"
The while I kiss the colder air in vain.

VIII

O love, how utterly am I bereaved
By Time, who sucks the honey of our days,
Sets sickle to our Aprils, and betrays
To killing winter all the sun achieved!
Our parted spirits are perplexed and grieved
Severed by cold, and change that never stays;
And what the clock, and what the season says
Is rumour neither valued nor believed.

Thus absence chills us to apparent death
And withers up our virtue, but together
We grow beyond vagaries of the weather
And make a summer of our mingled breath
Wherein we flourish, and forget to know
We must lie murdered by predestined snow.

IX

A subtle spirit has my path attended,
In likeness not a lion but a pard;
And when the arrows flew like hail, and hard,
He licked my wounds, and all my wounds were mended;
And happy I, who walked so well-defended,
With that translucid presence for a guard,
Under a sky reversed and evil-starred;
A woman by an archangel befriended.

Now must I end the knightly servitude
Which made him my preserver, and renounce
That heavenly aid forever and at once;
For it were neither courteous nor good
If we, who are but perishable things,
Should hang another weight between his wings.

X

When I perceive the sable of your hair
Silvered, and deep within those caverns are
Your eyesockets, a double-imaged star,
And your fine substance fretted down by care,
Then do I marvel that a woman dare
Prattle of mortal matters near and far
To one so wounded in demonic war
Against some prince of Sirius or Altair.

How is it possible that this hand of clay,
Though white as porcelain, can contrive a touch
So delicate it shall not hurt too much?

What voice can my invention find to say
So soft, precise, and scrupulous a word
You shall not take it for another sword?

XI

"Before I die, let me be happy here."
The glass of heaven was split, and by that token
I knew the bubble of my heart had broken;
The cool and chaste, the iridescent sphere,
Filled, in that vernal season of the year,
With sapling's blood, the beechen and the oaken
And the green willow's; when the word was spoken
This innocence did faint and disappear.

So have I lost my only wedding dower,
The veins of spring, enclosed within my heart,
Traced small in silver like a celestial chart;
And I am vanished in the leaf and flower,
Since, at your voice, my body's core and pith
Dissolves in air, and is destroyed forthwith.

XII

In our content, before the autumn came
To shower sallow droppings on the mould,
Sometimes you have permitted me to fold
Your grief in swaddling-bands, and smile to name
Yourself my infant, with an infant's claim
To utmost adoration as of old,
Suckled with kindness, fondled from the cold,
And loved beyond philosophy or shame.

I dreamt I was the mother of a son
Who had deserved a manger for a crib;
Torn from your body, furbished from your rib,
I am the daughter of your skeleton,
Born of your bitter and excessive pain:
I shall not dream you are my child again.

XIII

O mine is Psyche's heavy doom reversed
Who meet at noon, part by diminished light,
But never feel the subtle balm of night
Fall merciful upon a body pierced
By extreme love; and I considered first
That you, a god more prodigally bright
Than the lesser Eros, had enriched my sight,
Made your own morning, and the stars immersed.

But secondly I saw my soul arise
And, in the hushed obscure, presume to creep
Tiptoe upon your spirit laid asleep,
And slant the impious beam across your eyes;
And I believe I have my just deserts
Lacking the shadow of peace upon our hearts.

XIV

My fairer body and perfected spirit,
Beyond metempsychosis, and beyond
The faults you must forgive me to be fond,
Are yours in any death that I may merit;
Mortality has wearied us who wear it,
And they are wiser creatures who have shunned
The miry world, this slough of man's despond,
To fortify the skies we shall inherit.

I have entreated you to grant me Time
To memorize the pure appointed task;
Today it is Eternity I ask
In which to learn the lesson of this rhyme:
Its liberal periods are not too wide
To educate me fitly for your bride.

XV

My honoured lord, forgive the unruly tongue
That utters blasphemies; forgive the brain

Borne on a whirlwind of unhallowed pain:
Remember only the intrepid song;
The flag defended and the gauntlet flung;
The love that speech can never render plain;
The mind's resolve to turn and strive again;
The fortitude that has endured so long.

My cherished lord, in charity forgive
A starveling hope that may at times desire
To warm its frozen fingers at your fire;
'Tis by such trifles that your lovers live,
And so rise up, and in the starlight cold
Frighten the foxes from your loneliest fold.

XVI

I hereby swear that to uphold your house
I would lay my bones in quick destroying lime
Or turn my flesh to timber for all time;
Cut down my womanhood; lop off the boughs
Of that perpetual ecstasy that grows
From the heart's core; condemn it as a crime
If it be broader than a beam, or climb
Above the stature that your roof allows.

I am not the hearthstone nor the cornerstone
Within this noble fabric you have builded;
Not by my beauty was its cornice gilded;
Not on my courage were its arches thrown:
My lord, adjudge my strength, and set me where
I bear a little more than I can bear.

XVII

Upon your heart, which is the heart of all
My late discovered earth and early sky,
Give me the dearest privilege to die;
Your pity for the velvet of my pall;
Your patience for my grave's inviolate wall;
And for my passing bell, in passing by,

Your voice itself, diminished to a sigh
Above all other sounds made musical.

Meanwhile I swear to you I am content
To live without a sorrow to my name;
To live triumphant, and to die the same,
Upon the fringes of this continent,
This map of Paradise, this scrap of earth
Whereon you burn like flame upon a hearth.

XVIII

Let us leave talking of angelic hosts
Of nebulæ, and lunar hemispheres,
And what the days, and what the Uranian years
Shall offer us when you and I are ghosts;
Forget the festivals and pentecosts
Of metaphysics, and the lesser fears
Confound us, and seal up our eyes and ears
Like little rivers locked below the frosts.

And let us creep into the smallest room
That any hunted exile has desired
For him and for his love when he was tired;
And sleep oblivious of any doom
Which is beyond our reason to conceive;
And so forget to weep, forget to grieve,
And wake, and touch each other's hands, and turn
Upon a bed of juniper and fern.

Love Song

Forum, March 1929

Had I concealed my love
And you so loved me longer,
Since all the wise reprove
Confession of that hunger
In any human creature,
It had not been my nature.

I could not so insult
The beauty of that spirit
Who like a thunderbolt
Has broken me, or near it;
To love I have been candid,
Honest, and open-handed.

Although I love you well
And shall for ever love you,
I set that archangel
The depths of heaven above you;
And I shall lose you, keeping
His word, and no more weeping.

Chimæra Sleeping

Ah, lovely thing, I saw you lie
Within a beam of the sun's eye,
Where falling light and flying shade
Were bound together in a braid
Made of sky and earth colour:
Leaves blew over the forest floor:
The shadows were their noonday least.
I knew you neither man nor beast,
Nor god, nor rebel angel lost,
But that foreknown and holy ghost,
Beauty's pure pathetic shape;
The trap I never shall escape;
The heavenly bait; the honey breath
Issuing from the jaws of death.
So I approached, bereft of power,
And saw the pattern of a flower
Which moved in light and clearly shone
Under the arch of your breast-bone:
I saw a flower of white and green
Growing where your heart had been,
And grass obscured and dimly lit
As though a stream flowed over it:
Yea, through your body pale as glass
I saw the petals of the grass
Wave in the wind and softly stir
As seaweed under seawater.
You lay forlorn, hollow and thin
As a serpent's winter skin
From which his life of fiery gold
Has crawled away and left it cold:
And through your cold transparent flesh
The grass grew delicate and fresh;
I saw its blades, exact and plain
Through the blank crystal of your brain:
And nothing remained of fear and grief
Save the clear air and the green leaf;
And these the wind hath power to move;
And nothing there remained of love.

Then sorrow and joy dissolved my clay
To see you thus, and far away;
Your body laid upon the lawn;
Your spirit fled like a fox or fawn;
Your body consumed to silver ash
Whence passed the soul of the lightning flash;
Whence passed the lightning's living blood:
And I pursued you from the wood,
And, as I followed on, I wept
To leave the thicket where you slept.

Absent Thee From Felicity Awhile

"Spirits that walk beside me in the air—
Having laid by, in your impatience,
The bonds of body and sense—
Tell me how long I must forbear
The ecstasy of going hence
And still submit to wear
The mask of this pretence.

"Beloved creatures, who have left alone
Your sister in the ways you would not tread,
O excellent kind dead!
Have you forgot the burden of the bone?
The skull that clips my head
Is nowise lighter grown
Since your bright skins were shed."

Thus, upon middle earth, did I begin
My question, and the dead replied; "Submit:
Woman, who would be quit
Of this close panoply you walk within,
How ten times more unfit
Is his disguise, though worn threadbare and thin
By fire too fine for it!

"Consider who is your companion,
An hour obscured, but evident to our eyes,
Behind the slight disguise,
As light, and scarcely lesser than the sun;
Yet is he trapped within a skeleton
When even the transparent skies
Had clouded such an one.

"If you lament today, how must he faint
Between the ribs of stiff mortality?
Is it not plain to see
That heaven's own mind could not invent,
To clothe a river or a tree,

His soul's equivalent
Perfected in degree?

"O thank those stars, that even now are set
To grace the festival of your homecoming,
Like candles in a ring
About a board where friends are met,
That, upon earth, you found this subtle thing
Caught in the common net,
Beside you, wing to wing."

Felo de Se

My heart's delight, I must for love forget you;
I must put you from my heart, the better to please you;
I must make the power of the spirit set you
Beyond the power of the mind to seize you.

My dearest heart, in this last act of homage,
I must reject you; I must unlearn to love you;
I must make my eyes give up your adorable image
And from the inner chamber of my soul remove you.

Heart of my heart, the heart alone has courage
Thus to relinquish; it is yourself that stills you
In all my pulses, and dissolves the marriage
Of soul and soul, and at the heart's core kills you.

O Virtuous Light

A private madness has prevailed
Over the pure and valiant mind;
The instrument of reason failed
And the star-gazing eyes struck blind.

Sudden excess of light has wrought
Confusion in the secret place
Where the slow miracles of thought
Take shape through patience into grace.

Mysterious as steel and flint
The birth of this destructive spark
Whose inward growth has power to print
Strange suns upon the natural dark.

O break the walls of sense in half
And make the spirit fugitive!
This light begotten of itself
Is not a light by which to live!

The fire of farthing tallow dips
Dispels the menace of the skies
So it illuminate the lips
And enter the discerning eyes.

O virtuous light, if thou be man's
Or matter of the meteor stone,
Prevail against this radiance
Which is engendered of its own!

Hymn to Earth

Saturday Review of Literature, January 1929

Farewell, incomparable element,
Whence man arose, where he shall not return;
And hail, imperfect urn
Of his last ashes, and his firstborn fruit;
Farewell, the long pursuit,
And all the adventures of his discontent;
The voyages which sent
His heart averse from home:
Metal of clay, permit him that he come
To thy slow-burning fire as to a hearth;
Accept him as a particle of earth.

Fire, being divided from the other three,
It lives removed, or secret at the core;
Most subtle of the four,
When air flies not, nor water flows,
It disembodied goes,
Being light, elixir of the first decree,
More volatile than he;
With strength and power to pass
Through space, where never his least atom was:
He has no part in it, save as his eyes
Have drawn its emanation from the skies.

A wingless creature heavier than air,
He is rejected of its quintessence;
Coming and going hence,
In the twin minutes of his birth and death,
He may inhale as breath,
As breath relinquish heaven's atmosphere,
Yet in it have no share,
Nor can survive therein
Where its outer edge is filtered pure and thin:
It doth but lend its crystal to his lungs
For his early crying, and his final songs.

The element of water has denied
Its child; it is no more his element;
It never will relent;
Its silver harvests are more sparsely given
Than the rewards of heaven,
And he shall drink cold comfort at its side:
The water is too wide:
The seamew and the gull
Feather a nest made soft and pitiful
Upon its foam; he has not any part
In the long swell of sorrow at its heart.

Hail and farewell, beloved element,
Whence he departed, and his parent once;
See where thy spirit runs
Which for so long hath had the moon to wife;
Shall this support his life
Until the arches of the waves be bent
And grow shallow and spent?
Wisely it cast him forth
With his dead weight of burdens nothing worth,
Leaving him, for the universal years,
A little seawater to make his tears.

Hail, element of earth, receive thy own,
And cherish, at thy charitable breast,
This man, this mongrel beast:
He ploughs the sand, and, at his hardest need,
He sows himself for seed;
He ploughs the furrow, and in this lies down
Before the corn is grown;
Between the apple bloom
And the ripe apple is sufficient room
In time, and matter, to consume his love
And make him parcel of a cypress grove.

Receive him as thy lover for an hour
Who will not weary, by a longer stay,

The kind embrace of clay;
Even within thine arms he is dispersed
To nothing, as at first;
The air flings downward from its four-quartered tower
Him whom the flames devour;
At the full tide, at the flood,
The sea is mingled with his salty blood:
The traveller dust, although the dust be vile,
Sleeps as thy lover for a little while.

This Corruptible

Ladies Home Journal, April 1929

The Body, long oppressed
And pierced, then prayed for rest
(Being but apprenticed to the other Powers);
And kneeling in that place
Implored the thrust of grace
Which makes the dust lie level with the flowers.

Then did that fellowship
Of three, the Body strip;
Beheld his wounds, and none among them mortal;
The Mind severe and cool;
The Heart still half a fool;
The fine-spun Soul, a beam of sun can startle.

These three, a thousand years
Had made adventurers
Amid all villainies the earth can offer,
Applied them to resolve
From the universal gulph
What pangs the poor material flesh may suffer.

"This is a pretty pass;
To hear the growing grass
Complain; the clay cry out to be translated;
Will not this grosser stuff
Receive reward enough
If stabled after labouring, and baited?"

Thus spoke the Mind in scorn:
The Heart, which had outworn
The Body, and was weary of its fashion,
Preferring to be dressed
In skin of bird or beast,
Replied more softly, in a feigned compassion.

"Anatomy most strange
Crying to chop and change;
Inferior copy of a higher image;
While I, the noble guest,
Sick of your second-best
Sigh for embroidered archangelic plumage:

"For shame, thou fustian cloak!"
And then the Spirit spoke;
Within the void it swung securely tethered
By strings composed of cloud;
It spoke both low and loud
Above a storm no lesser star had weathered.

"O lodging for the night!
O house of my delight!
O lovely hovel builded for my pleasure!
Dear tenement of clay
Endure another day
As coffin sweetly fitted to my measure.

"Take Heart, and call to Mind
Although we are unkind;
Although we steal your shelter, strength, and clothing;
'Tis you who shall escape
In some enchanting shape
Or be dissolved to elemental nothing.

"You, the unlucky slave,
Are the lily on the grave;
The wave that runs above the bones a-whitening;
You are the new-mown grass;
And the wheaten bread of the Mass;
And the fabric of the rain, and the lightning.

"If one of us elect
To leave the poor suspect

Imperfect bosom of the earth our parent;
And from the world avert
The Spirit or the Heart
Upon a further and essential errand;

"His chain he cannot slough
Nor cast his substance off;
He bears himself upon his flying shoulder;
The Heart, infirm and dull;
The Mind, in any skull;
Are captive still, and wearier and colder.

"'Tis you who are the ghost,
Disintegrated, lost;
The burden shed; the dead who need not bear it;
O grain of God in power,
Endure another hour!
It is but for an hour," said the Spirit.

Fair Annet's Song

One thing comes and another thing goes:
Frosts in November drive away the rose;
Like a blowing ember the windflower blows
And drives away the snows.

It is sad to remember and sorrowful to pray:
Let us laugh and be merry, who have seen today
The last of the cherry and the first of the may;
And neither one will stay.

Hughie at the Inn

Is it not fine to fling against loaded dice
Yet to win once or twice?
To bear a rusty sword without an edge
Yet wound the thief in the hedge?
To be unhorsed, and drown in horrid muck,
And in at the death, by luck?
To meet a masked assassin in a cape
And kill him, and escape?
To have the usurers all your fortune take,
And a bare living make
By industry, and your brow's personal sweat?
To be caught in the bird-net
Of a bad marriage; then to be trepanned
And stranded on foreign land?
To be cast into a prison damp and vile,
And break bars, with a blunt file?
To be cut down from gallows while you breathe
And live, by the skin of your teeth?
To defy the tyrant world, and at a pinch
To wrest from it an inch?
To engage the stars in combat, and therefrom
Pluck a hair's breadth of room?
Is it not fine, worthy of Titans or gods,
To challenge such heavy odds?
But no, but no, my lad;
'Tis cruel chance gone mad;
A stab in the back, a serpent in the breast;
And worst that murders best.
Such broad and open affronts to fear and pain
Breed maggots in the brain;
They are not valour, but the merest rash
Rubbish and balderdash.
Fortune's a drab, and vice her native soil,
And the button's off her foil.
Season your ale, now these long nights draw in,
With thought to save your skin:
Be provident, and pray for cowardice
And the loaded pair of dice.

Nonsense Rhyme

Whatever's good or bad or both
Is surely better than the none;
There's grace in either love or loathe;
Sunlight, or freckles on the sun.

The worst and best are both inclined
To snap like vixens at the truth;
But, O, beware the middle mind
That purrs and never shows a tooth!

Beware the smooth ambiguous smile
That never pulls the lips apart;
Salt of pure and pepper of vile
Must season the extremer heart.

A pinch of fair, a pinch of foul.
And bad and good make best of all;
Beware the moderated soul
That climbs no fractional inch to fall.

Reason's a rabbit in a hutch,
And ecstasy's a were-wolf ghost;
But, O, beware the nothing-much
And welcome madness and the most!

Bread Alone

Let not the heart's intention
To be both brave and good
Cheat that devoted engine
Of spiritual food.

Because it is not cruel,
Because it is not great,
Provide it fire, and fuel
Sufficient for its state.

Ah, poor machine, and faithful,
That limps without a wing!
My love, be never wrathful
With this imperfect thing.

Farewell, Sweet Dust

Now I have lost you, I must scatter
All of you on the air henceforth;
Not that to me it can ever matter
But it's only fair to the rest of earth.

Now especially, when it is winter
And the sun's not half so bright as he was,
Who wouldn't be glad to find a splinter
That once was you, in the frozen grass?

Snowflakes, too, will be softer feathered
Clouds, perhaps, will be whiter plumed;
Rain, whose brilliance you caught and gathered,
Purer silver have reassumed.

Farewell, sweet dust; I was never a miser:
Once, for a minute, I made you mine:
Now you are gone, I am none the wiser
But the leaves of the willow are bright as wine.

To a Lady's Countenance

This unphilosophic sight;
This silly mask of silken white;
This thing which has, to hide its grief,
Less than a rose's lesser leaf;
This web a spider might have spun
With patience and precision;
This veil concealing sorrow's face,
Arranged with coquetry and grace,
Which shall remain, when all is said,
After sorrow itself is dead;
In colour, a camellia flower;
In shape, a whim of the glass-blower;
The mind's eye hollowed and made blind,
But not the brow above the mind;
And, whatsoever may be starved,
The little lips uncut, uncarved;
God's power has disdained to mould
This clay so delicate and cold;
Perchance he took it for the flesh
Of mushrooms, or the silkworm's mesh;
Stuff too slight to bear the fine
Finger-tip of the divine
In lines of noble heritage;
And so, you do not show your age.

Little Elegy

Withouten you
No rose can grow;
No leaf be green
If never seen
Your sweetest face;
No bird have grace
Or power to sing;
Or anything
Be kind, or fair,
And you nowhere.

CHAPTER SIX

From *Collected Poems of Elinor Wylie* —Hitherto Uncollected Poems

New York: Alfred A. Knopf, 1932

Green Hair

I know you wonder why I wear
The hat which I have called Green Hair
And why I cover up my own
Which has a tawny chestnut tone
Warm, when all its lights are lit,
As a swarm of bees with the sun on it.
You say bronze hair is prettier
Than this strange green of feathery fur;
But there's a charm in this strange green
Which is so nearly blue; I've seen
A comb of coral set with pearls
Drawn through lengths of such green curls
In the green gloom of a chilly cave
Down, far down in a hollow wave;
And under ancient forest trees
Long green tresses such as these
Shadow like a falling veil
Shy secret faces, dusky pale;
And I have seen green locks like those
Deep in a glacier, under snows.
I have seen such green hair tossed
From the brows of a creature wandering lost
On the other side of a waning moon,
And in the golden sun at noon
I have seen young April plait
Flowers in showery hair like that,
And wring the rain from it in drops,
And spread it to dry on green hill-tops.
Now do you wonder that I wear
The hat which I have called Green Hair?
Thus with witchcraft I am crowned
And wrapped in marvels round and round;
There's sorcery in it, and surprise;
Believe your own dark-amber eyes
When mine of hazel look at you
Turned to incredible turquoise blue.

Pretty Words

Bookman, October 1921

Poets make pets of pretty, docile words:
I love smooth words, like gold-enamelled fish
Which circle slowly with a silken swish,
And tender ones, like downy-feathered birds:
Words shy and dappled, deep-eyed deer in herds,
Come to my hand, and playful if I wish,
Or purring softly at a silver dish,
Blue Persian kittens, fed on cream and curds.

I love bright words, words up and singing early;
Words that are luminous in the dark, and sing;
Warm lazy words, white cattle under trees;
I love words opalescent, cool, and pearly,
Like midsummer moths, and honied words like bees,
Gilded and sticky, with a little sting.

A Courtesy

Harper's, June 1925

Having conceived that this delight alone
Must be the corner stone
For all my building; having stripped it bare
Of you and found it fair;
Having accepted deprivation;
I have knelt down to bow
My brow upon the brow
Of granite; I have filled my empty hand
With running pulse of sand,
And twined my fingers in a bough of leaves;
I have pushed back my sleeves
To let the water twist
Its coolness round my wrist,
And I have kissed the comfortable moss
For cushioning a cross
Of racking timber sharp as childbirth bed;
I have embraced instead
Of love, a ponderable cloud of rain.

Let us return again
Together; let us kneel upon the grass
In quiet clear as glass,
Bending stiff necks and crooking stubborn knees
In courteous obsequies
For that poor wolf, but late mistitled Pride;
Let us be thankful that this beast has died,
And thankful for the silence of the trees,
As I was thankful for the cheer I had
To hear their chattering when I was sad.

Golden Bough

New York Evening Post, December 1923

These lovely groves of fountain-trees that shake
A burning spray against autumnal cool
Descend again in molten drops to make
The rutted path a river and a pool.

They rise in silence, fall in quietude,
Lie still as looking-glass to every sense
Save where their lion-colour in the wood
Roars to miraculous heat and turbulence.

Portrait in Black Paint, With a Very Sparing Use of Whitewash

New Yorker, March 1927

"She gives herself;" there's a poetic thought;
She gives you comfort sturdy as a reed;
She gives you fifty things you might have bought,
And half a hundred that you'll never need;
She gives you friendship, but it's such a bother
You'd fancy influenza from another.

She'd give the shirt from off her back, except that
She doesn't wear a shirt, and most men do;
And often and most bitterly she's wept that
A starving tramp can't eat a silver shoe,
Or some poor beggar, slightly alcoholic,
Enjoy with Donne a metaphysical frolic.

She gives away her darling secret hope
At dinner tables between eight and nine,
And she would give Saint Peter's to the Pope,
And coals to men of Newcastle-on-Tyne,
She would arrange a match for Solomon
Or give Casanova an adoptive son.

She does not give advice; that I admit;
Here's her sole virtue, and I'll count it double,
Forgiving her some crime because of it,
But she gives tiresome and endless trouble.
If you need rest, she'll straight contrive a racket;
If gaiety, she'll fetch a padded jacket.

And she gives love of the least useful kind
At which advanced civilization mocks;
Half, a Platonic passion of the mind,
And half, a mad desire to mend the socks;
She's always wishing to turn back the page
And live with children in a golden age.

She gives a false impression that she's pretty
Because she has a soft, deceptive skin
Saved from her childhood; yet it seems a pity
That she should be as vain of this as sin;
Her mind might bloom, she might reform the world
In those lost hours while her hair is curled.

She gives a vague impression that she's lazy,
But when she writes she grows intense and thorough;
Gone quietly and ecstatically crazy
Among the sea-blue hills of Peterboro;
She'll work within her cool, conventual flat
As self-sufficient as a Persian cat.

And she can live on aspirin and Scotch
Or British ginger beer and bread and butter,
And like them both, and neither very much;
And in her infancy she possessed a stutter
Which gives a strong impression that she's shy
When heard today, and this is verity.

But when she clothes herself in gold and silver
In the evening, she gives herself away;
Having remained a high, laborious delver
For all the hours of a sunny day,
At night she gives you rather the idea
Of mad Ophelia tutored by Medea.

She gives you nothing worth consideration;
The effervescence of enthusiasm
Is trivial stuff; she'll give you adoration
If you belong to her peculiar schism;
As, that a certain English man of letters
Need never call the Trinity his betters.

Sometimes she gives her heart; sometimes instead
Her tongue's sharp side. Her will is quick to soften.
She has no strength of purpose in her head

And she gives up entirely too often;
Her manners mingle in disastrous ways
"The Lower Depths" and the Court of Louis Seize.

Doubtless, she gives her enemies the creeps
And all her friends a vast amount of worry;
She's given oblivion only when she sleeps;
She says she loves the grave; but she'd be sorry
To die, while it is vanity to live;
"She gives herself;" what has she left to give?

She'd give her eyes—but both her eyes are blind—
And her right hand—but both her hands are weak—
To be "Careless to win, unskilled to find,
And quick–and quick–to lose what all men seek."
But whether this has truly been her story
She'll never know, this side of purgatory.

Ejaculation

In this short interval to tear
The living words from dying air,
To pull them to me, quick and brave
As swordfish from a silver wave,
To drag them dripping, cold and salt
To suffocation in this vault
The which a lid of vapour shuts,
To shake them down like hazel-nuts
Or golden acorns from an oak
Whose twigs are flame above the smoke,
To snatch them suddenly from dust
Like apples flavoured with the frost
Of mountain valleys marble-cupped,
To leap to them and interrupt
Their flight that cleaves the atmosphere
As white and arrowy troops of deer
Divide the forest,—make my words
Like feathers torn from living birds!

An American in England

Saturday Review of Literature, October 1930

Here Is a Marvel, and No God May Ban It.
An Olive Branch, Grown in New England Granite.

I love every stock and stone
Of this land, no more my own;
Which we lost, that it might be
Wider by half a world of sea;
We cleft the rock with bitter toil
Having left our roots in sweeter soil,
Or torn them up and bid them thrive
Like mandrakes, bloody but alive:
Dust and sweat were wholesome salves
Until our hearts were cut in halves.
Ah, that was a prodigious wound;
A severing of sacred ground;
That was bad; but this is best;
Let the uprooted mandrake rest.
Love the good and leave the fault;
Sow not his several graves with salt;
Sow not these graves with dragon's teeth;
Part of England lies beneath
Both the granite and the loam:
Let the divided heart come home
To half-content, and understand
His passion for a wilder land
Still untamed and still unfed
By flesh and bone that England bred.
If we desert the deed undone
Alas, what daughter and what son!
Break the sword: the iron strike
To plough-shares, share and share alike!

Letter to V——

No, V——, you never will persuade me
That Death is other than a friend;
I can't believe the hand that made me
Shall so unmake me in the end.

Suppose a Holy Ghost or Spirit
Came dressed in red instead of white;
A child may see some such, and fear it
On Christmas Eve or Christmas night.

It's not a Dustman or a Reaper;
It's not a wormy skeleton;
Perhaps the dark disguise is deeper
But It's the Father or the Son.

You will not look, because you dassn't,
At what is hidden in His bag;
I know it is another Present;
Eagle's wing or skin of stag.

They call it Future, but it isn't;
It is the Present when it come;
And shall the swinging fruit be wizened?
And shall the singing bird be dumb?

You know, upon our birthday mornings,
They gave us pretty hair and eyes;
Why should our lives' entire earnings
Be less than excrement of flies?

It's not because I've had so little;
It is because I've had so much
That I believe that clay and spittle
Contain the soul of Such and Such

The secret—and He has not told it—
Is that which here escapes us most;

And, even though we try to hold it,
It shall not finally be lost.

Although they burn me on a faggot
I turn me to my Father's house;
I will not have Him called a Maggot;
I will not have Him called a Louse.

I will not have Him called a Nothing;
I'll love Him, and I'll lay me down,
In silver coverlid and clothing,
Beside my brother, Thomas Browne.

And, while I live, I'll call Him *Mighty,*
Yea, and *Eloquent* and *Just;*
And scratch in earth: *Integer Vitæ;*
And: *Dolce Mors* upon the dust.

The Pebble

Saturday Review of Literature, January 1929

If any have a stone to shy,
Let him be David and not I;
The lovely shepherd, brave and vain,
Who has a maggot in the brain,
Which, since the brain is bold and pliant,
Takes the proportions of a giant.
Alas, my legendary fate!
Who sometimes rage, but never hate.
Long, long before the pebble flieth
I see a virtue in Goliath;
Yea, in the Philistine his face,
A touching majesty and grace;
Then like the lights of evening shine
The features of the Philistine
Until my spirit faints to see
The beauty of my enemy.
If any have a stone to fling
Let him be a shepherd-king,
Who is himself so beautiful
He may detest the gross and dull
With holy rage and heavenly pride
To make a pebble sanctified
And feather its course with wings of scorn;
But, from the day that I was born
Until like corn I bow to the sickle,
I am in hatred false and fickle.
I am most cruel to anyone
Who hates me with devotion;
I will not freeze, I will not burn;
I make his heart a poor return
For all the passion that he spends
In swearing we shall never be friends;
For all the pains his passion spent
In hatred I am impotent;
The sad perversity of my mind
Sees in him my kin and kind.

Alas, my shameful heritage,
False in hate and fickle in rage!
Alas, to lack the power to loathe!
I like them each; I love them both;
Philistine and shepherd-king
They strike the pebble from my sling;
My heart grows cold, my spirit grows faint;
Behold, a hero and a saint
Where appeared, a moment since,
A giant and a heathen prince;
And I am bound and given over
To be no better than a lover.
Alas, who strove as a holy rebel!
They have broke my sling and stole my pebble:
If any have a stone to throw
It is not I, ever or now.

Sonnet

You are the faintest freckles on the hide
Of fawns; the hoofprint stamped into the slope
Of slithering glaciers by the antelope;
The silk upon the mushroom's under side
Constricts you, and your eyelashes are wide
In pools uptilted on the hills; you grope
For swings of water twisted to a rope
Over a ledge where amber pebbles glide.

Shelley perceived you on the Caucasus;
Blake prisoned you in glassy grains of sand
And Keats in goblin jars from Samarcand;
Poor Coleridge found you in a poppy-seed;
But you escape the clutching most of us,
Shaped like a ghost, and imminent with speed.

Sonnet

How many faults you might accuse me of
Are truth, and by my truthfulness admitted!
A fool, perhaps, how many caps had fitted,
How many motleys clothed me like a glove.
Thriftless of gold and prodigal of love;
Fanatical in pride, and feather-witted
In the world's business; if your tongue had spitted
Such frailties, they were possible to prove.

But you have hit the invulnerable joint
In this poor armour patched from desperate fears;
This is the breastplate that you cannot pierce,
That turns and breaks your most malicious point;
This strict ascetic habit of control
That industry has woven for my soul.

CHAPTER SEVEN

From *Last Poems of Elinor Wylie*

New York: Alfred A. Knopf, 1943
Reprint; Chicago: Academy Chicago, 1982

Beltane

Under oak, ash and thorn
My soul was born.
Under thorn, oak and ash
My body bent to the lash.
Under ash, thorn and oak
My heart broke.
Under oak, ash and thorn all three
I was nailed to a tree.

From the Wall

Woman, be steel against loving, enfold and defend you,
Turn from the innocent look and the arrogant tongue;
You shall be coppery dross to the purses that spend you;
Lock up your years like a necklace of emeralds strung.

Lock up your heart like a jewel; be cruel and clever;
Woman, be strong against loving, be iron, be stone;
Never and never and never and never and never
Give for the tears of a lover a tear of your own.

Cover the clutch of your greed with a velvety gloving;
Take from the good if you can, from the vile if you must;
Take from the proud and alone, from the cowardly loving;
Hold out your hands for the pity; accept of the lust.

Silver Bells and Cockle Shells

Once I fled as children flee
Far from my desire;
Then my freedom was to me
As Promethean fire.

I fell in with something dark;
Something like a man;
Then I took my Titan-spark,
Turned about and ran.

Drinking fire's delicious dew,
Dancing like a star,
On I flew, on I flew,
Far and very far.

I fell in with someone kind,
And he gave me gloves,
Lovely cloaks with ermine lined,
Several kind of loves.

In his arms I learned to sleep,
From his hand I fed,
Till I left my friend to weep;
Far away I fled.

Tasting air's enchanting speed
Far I fled away,
Till I found a bitter need
On a rainy day.

I fell in with someone good
Standing in the rain,
Gave me kisses, gave me food
Sweet as manna-grain.

In his arms I learned to rest;
Took his sugar-bread,

Till I left my lover's breast;
Far away I fled.

Do I flee, loving flight?
Do I flee to find
Something lost, something light,
Something half-unkind?

Written on the Flyleaf of John Webster's Plays

Having so long walked hand in hand with Hell
I find these gentry little less than kin;
I speak their sulphurous language; we begin
Straightway to cap each other's jests, and tell
Fantastical adventures which befell
At midnight, some eccentric court within—
Where fiery anger plotted with pale sin—
Crime's sanctuary, murder's citadel.

Fouler the cruelties which desecrate
These later days, to poison heart and mind,
And strangle, with the bloody hand of Hate,
The thrice-stabbed soul; from such I turn to find
The black Calabrian comrade in my fate,
And Corombona, as a sister, kind.

Little Joke

Stripping an almond tree in flower
  The wise apothecary's skill
A single drop of lethal power
  From perfect sweetness can distill.

From bitterness in efflorescence,
  With murderous poisons packed therein;
The poet draws pellucid essence
  Pure as a drop of metheglin.

CHAPTER EIGHT

Poems Only in Periodicals

Seven Basketsful for Louis Untermeyer

Saturday Review of Literature, November 1927

If he asked her for bread and she gave him a scone,
Strike me dead if it is not the Sassenach tone.
I have said, may St. Andrew have mercy upon her;
If she gave me such bread she would give me a scunner.
By the reverend head of each bishop and don,
By the martyr that bled, by the Abbot of Scone,
By St. Leonard, St. Michael, John Knox, and St. John,
If you ask her for bread she should give you a scone.
For sweet Charity's sake, for myself and my erring
If I ask for a snake may I get caller herring!

Anti-feminist Song, for My Sister

New Yorker, February 1929

Each of us, born every minute,
  Still wears fern-seed in her shoes;
Love of man, we always win it;
  Peace of mind, we always lose.

Drawing cheques is still our pastime;
  Paying checks our private hell;
No good swearing it's the last time
  While we know ourselves so well!

I am I, and you, my darling,
  Someone very like myself;
Hear the back-door wolf a-snarling
  For bread and cheese upon the shelf!

Well, and let him lick our platters!
  Let him drain our loving-cups!
Do we really think it matters
  Save as Cerberus his sops?

Ah, from such the rats have scampered
  Who give all, but not a damn!
How the wind remains ill-tempered
  To the thoroughly-shorn lamb!

Yes, we've had our fairly thick times
  Paying for the cakes and beers:
It's more fun to be the victims
  Than the bloody conquerors.

Prose

75-1194
75c
A BOOK-OF-THE-MONTH CLUB SELECTION
IN ITS ORIGINAL ALFRED A. KNOPF EDITION
The Orphan Angel
A NOVEL BY ELINOR WYLIE
A magnificent historical novel— and something more . . .
"Brilliant . . . Mrs. Wylie's masterpiece"
—The New York Times

CHAPTER NINE

From *Jennifer Lorn: A Sedate Extravaganza. Illuminating Episodes in the Lives of the Hon. Gerald Poynyard and His Bride. Complete herein in Three Books*

New York: George H. Doran Company, 1923
London: Grant Richards, 1924
Collected Prose of Elinor Wylie. New York: Alfred A. Knopf, 1933

Book One: Gerald

1. A Gross of Brass Knockers

When Warren Hastings became Governor-General of India in the year 1773, he had among his associates a young man whose abilities, if somewhat less than those of his chief, were so peculiarly marked that Hastings soon found it necessary to decide whether this person was to be broken as an enemy or raised to the illustrious eminence of a friend. Having fixed upon the latter course, the great man never regretted his choice, and the able associate was content to remain just that and nothing more, knowing full well that though under other circumstances he might himself have joined the perilous and thinning ranks of great men, his own position was far safer and only a little less lucrative in the long run.

The Honourable Gerald Poynyard was the heir to a barony whose extreme antiquity was the only satisfactory thing about it, and at an early age he made up his mind finally and firmly that the other satisfactory things of life were so essential to his happiness that he could even bring himself to work, and to work hard, in order to obtain them. In his day and generation, this was an idea so original and surprising that Gerald, at one time, came very near to being regarded as the black sheep of an otherwise respectable family, but his almost immediate acquisition of vast sums of money did much to remove this prejudice from the minds of his more critical aunts and cousins.

The natural question raised by these gentry was, "Why doesn't Gerald make a good match?" but to this he had always the same answer: "Because I happen to want a beautiful wife." Suggestions that beauty and money might sometimes be found in exquisitely balanced portions he pooh-poohed, reminding his relatives that the smallness of his estates and the largeness of his nose forbade any such plan unless he was willing to make a victim of some romantic ward in Chancery, or discover a banker's daughter who weighed in at less than thirteen stone. His father, having no choice whatever in the matter, gave in with a good grace, and let the boy have his own way, remarking only that since decent class distinctions seemed to count for nothing in Gerald's estimation, it was a pity that he was tossing aside a splendid career in the diplomatic service to become a clerk in the East India Company.

Gerald considered his three years at Cambridge sadly wasted; he took a deep interest in Greek History and nourished a secret passion for mathematics, but on the whole his university career was a mere marking of time, chiefly memorable for the extreme pleasure he took in the Newmarket Races and for several visits to the continent during the Long Vacation. During these visits he perfected his knowledge of French; it was customary among his friends to say that Gerald's accent was the best possible earnest of the stainless aristocracy of his acquaintance in that delightful country. As early as 1765 he was a familiar figure at the more exclusive coffee-houses in London; he possessed a sort of cold and deadly skill at gaming, seldom exercised, but almost never without success.

In this same year, when he was barely twenty, he first appeared at Versailles, where his odd but distinguished type won him a decided measure of appreciation from the various societies into which the good offices of his connections easily introduced him. Perhaps these connections still hoped that he would have the wisdom to select a wife from among Parisian banking circles rather than to haunt the court in a determined pursuit of knowledge of the morals and manners of the *haute noblesse* of France; if so they were disappointed. He was polite to the bankers and tax farmers; they found him charming, and honoured his small draughts with real pleasure, but he never looked at the daughters' faces however gallantly he bowed over their hands. At the court he deliberately attached himself to certain ladies of great but diminishing beauty; as they were all at least twenty years older than he they possibly knew more about the ways of the world than he did at the beginning of their association; it is certain that at the end what little he did not understand about life at the French court could have been written upon the proverbial sixpence.

At Versailles he was accepted without question as a young and clever Englishman of good family; his great height, the prominence of his pale blue eyes, and his thin bony nose satisfied the recognised conception of an Englishman, and with the help of a fair skin, and thick hair shining flaxen under the powder, he passed for handsome. Agreeable he undoubtedly was; highly agreeable, with perfect manners, not too strikingly in evidence, and a wit just subtle and serene enough to please those most captious critics. He had a fine figure, and when he had money he was generous with it. Altogether, he was rather more than liked. There is a spirited portrait of him in one of Voltaire's most famous letters, written at this time. He is introduced as "a young Englishman, truly intelligent." This, from Voltaire, is much, but no more than the truth.

Upon attaining his majority, Gerald immediately applied for and received the position of clerk in the East India Company. The consternation of his family has already been dwelt upon; it is only necessary to add that his creditable record at the University, and his really brilliant successes at Versailles made the blow all the more crushing. When he left Cambridge, the preceding year, his most influential cousin had informed him that the Diplomatic Service might have been founded for no other purpose than to give scope to his indisputable talents; even going so far as to state, in a stage whisper, that he was practically authorized to offer him a small but honorable post at the court of Saxony. Gerald asked what stipend he might expect, and on being enlightened as to what his cousin assured him was an unimportant point, sniffed loudly and disdainfully. A year later he was in Calcutta.

Gerald, who loved all courts except the smaller German ones, was now in a counting-house, but he had reached the counting-house by way of many courts, amusing and various as the jewelled stars and ribbons which they had bestowed upon this young and ingratiating foreigner. Following a week of amazing luck at White's, the results of which were augmented by a modest, but timely, bequest from an adoring old nurse, he discovered that he was in possession of sufficient funds to travel at least part of the way to India in the proper style for the Grand Tour; while he traversed Europe by the lengthy and circuitous route of his own choosing he was in all respects the young nobleman setting forth to see the world. This curious circumstance, taken in conjunction with the fact that the same sum of money invested in the business of a merchant in Spanish wines or a new and progressive banking house in the City would have given Gerald a tiny but assured income for the rest of his life, might lead the ignorant to suspect him of profligacy and extravagance. This was not the case; he was simply investing the money in himself, with a nice appreciation of his own powers. By the time Gerald took ship at Marseilles, his brocades and velvets were wearing threadbare and his purse was exceedingly depleted, but he had polished his French *ad unguem,* and given the last perfect twist to his swordsmanship; improved the soundness of his chess in Germany and heightened its brilliance in Italy; shot bears in the Pyrenees with Spanish peasants and sharpened his steely wit against the best brains in Europe. After buying a complete outfit at the proper shops in Marseilles, an outfit including such delicate linens and nankeen that he shuddered to contemplate them in the aguish grip of the *mistral* under a sky which set his teeth on edge, he spent his every penny on chincona bark, six dozen bottles of the finest brandy, and the works of Voltaire bound in dark rose-colored morocco and having his own arms blind-tooled on the covers at an extra cost of twelve louis. Then he boarded an East Indiaman, and, passing Gibraltar under a tiger-striped December sunset, looked his last on British soil until he landed on a mud bank in the Hoogli.

He had made all the necessary arrangements with the East India Company; aboard the ship his passage had been taken for him, and the voyage passed pleasantly enough. His fellow passengers were dull in the extreme; a sandy-haired Scotchman, going out to the same counting-house in Calcutta, was soon driven to saturnine and scornful silence by Gerald's godless conversation; two ingenuous youths, destined for military service in the Sepoy army of the Company, began by assuming airs of superiority and ended in a state of abject fear which threw them into paroxysms of laughter at the subtlest and most abstruse of his jokes, which they invariably failed to comprehend and which were invariably directed against themselves. The Scotchman often wanted to laugh, but his conscience forbade. Gerald would have been wretched without the brandy and *Candide;* with the help of these the long blue days and black silver nights melted away like a dream.

When he woke in the counting-house, he was very wide awake indeed; he was greedy for work, tireless, watchful, terrible with a sort of guarded and restrained passion. He was quickly promoted. As he rose his associates came to fear him. The Scotchman, Macallister, maintained that he was the devil, and Macallister feared him less than the others did. Oddly enough, the natives adored him; in dealing with them he always drew the velvet glove over the exceeding hardness of his hand, but the same hand was there, the same texture and weight of iron. Going out in 1766, at the age of twenty-one, he was from the first a marked man; his aristocratic connections and his striking appearance probably contributed to his success, but in the main it was the result of sheer ability and the cold and enduring determination to encompass certain ends. His health was astonishing; during his seven years as an employé of the East India Company he lost every scrap of fat with which European cooking had padded his bones; his freckled face grew as yellow as his hair; his predatory hands were claws, and yet he was never ill, never even tired; he combined the work of a navvy and a prime minister, and throve upon it. Soon he was the recognised ambassador to the more peevish of the native princes, his perfect firmness and impeccable suavity made him invaluable to the Company and acceptable to the most pampered of rajahs. Here was a man who had every grace, every accomplishment; a man whose chess was as magnificent as his marksmanship; a man who could manage a horse or a political intrigue with light and masterly touch; a man who had no fear and who was beginning to have a great deal of money.

2. The Earl's Elzevir

Jennifer Lorn was the most beautiful girl in Devonshire; indeed, with the possible exception of a few Genoese and Sicilian peasants and a shawled colleen or two in Galway, she was the most beautiful girl in the world. At this time she was exactly seventeen years old; as her father preferred to spend his money upon first editions there is no contemporary portrait of her in existence; the vision of her early loveliness faded from reality like dew licked up by the sun. The miniature which Gerald ordered in Paris a year later was destroyed during the Revolution; its owner had not the heart to claim it on his return from the East in 1773, and it remained in the artist's hands for twenty years before Fouquier-Tinville chanced to see it lying in the blood and mud of the streets; because it smiled so innocently at him he ground it under his boot. As the old miniature painter's head had just fallen into the basket, the incident appeared unimportant at the time, but now it seems a pity that the little ivory oval did not survive the Reign of Terror, as by all accounts it must have been not only an excellent likeness but a delicate and distinguished work of art.

The daughter of the Earl of Tam-Linn and the Honourable Clarinda Cleverly-Neville, Jennifer was almost bound to be a beauty, but no one could have foreseen the remarkable success with which she contrived to fuse and combine the good looks of both families into an exquisite concord quite her own. Tam-Linn was now nearing seventy; he was still an extremely handsome man; a lean Scot, tall and proud and very fierce, with bright eyes and bright red hair as yet hardly dimmed by grey. Jennifer had taken his eyes and hair and made them more amazing; she had taken as much of his height as she needed, and the scornful lift of his forehead, and his long throat, and his slenderness. But she had rejected his harsh burring voice; she had rejected his nervous energy and a good half of his brains. From her mother she had chosen a charming languor, a complexion of rose and cream, little bones, and soft flesh to lie sparingly over them; her hands and feet were her mother's, and so were her laziness and her good nature. She had her mother's minute teeth and extravagant eyelashes; if she had ever grown plump she would have had her mother's dimples too, but the Lorn blood running wild and chilly in her veins kept her thin and clear as green leaves in April.

Besides her beauty, she had all manner of engaging tricks and traits; people smiled when she spoke, and the more susceptible, seeing her praying in church on Sunday, were not infrequently moved to tears. But she was neither very strong nor very clever; the suave warm air of Devon tended to increase her natural lassitude, and none of her governesses had taught her more than the use of the globes, a little music, and the ability to converse unintelligently in French and German. However, her accent in each language was beyond reproach; her singing voice, a strange little muffled contralto, had been so far neglected that it remained quite adorable, and her touch upon the spinet was too light and casual to be really distressing. She was excessively fond of sitting upon a garden seat and reading Bishop Percy's Reliques; she would have preferred to lie down in the grass under the shade of the copper beeches, but this was forbidden owing to the supposed delicacy of Cleverly-Neville chests, long her mother's excuse for protracted absences from Carterhaugh. This lady shared her daughter's taste for poetry, but she was perfectly satisfied with garden seats and the works of Mr. Gray and Mr. Goldsmith; she was much more intellectual than Jennifer, and a valued friend of Sir Horace Walpole's. In her youth she had been romantic; to marry Tam-Linn was a more adventurous manner of indulging a passion for Scotch history than a mere reading of Bishop Percy's ballads. In her early married life she had found Caxton's Malory among her husband's books and forthwith insisted that her infant daughter should be christened Guinevere in the parish church of Cleverly-Neville; Tam-Linn insisted that the child should be baptised by the minister at Carterhaugh, and given the name of Janet; they compromised upon Jennifer, an old Neville name. A journey to Scotland during a particularly wet April proved impossible under the circumstances, but Tam-Linn was allowed to call his daughter Jenny.

The more robust of her Carterhaugh cousins called her Jenny Forlorn; her mother was accustomed to dress her in white muslin all the year round, and this habit, though highly satisfactory from an æsthetic point of view, produced during the Scotch winters a type of sore throat which did not tend to raise the spirits. Lady Tam-Linn saw her chance and took it; Jennifer's health could not possibly support so severe a climate except for the month of August. Lady Tam-Linn was happier in Devon; Jennifer was happier in Devon; Tam-Linn himself was happier in Devon after his wife had the most valuable portion of his library, including all his classical manuscripts and every Elzevir he possessed, removed to Cleverly-Neville. He stayed at Carterhaugh from the beginning of August until he joined his family at Christmas; his sons sometimes stayed with him, and his daughter sometimes wished she could. Had she done so, and joined the other Lorn and Carterhaugh girls in their racing and chasing over the moor, it is probable that her vitality would have been higher; it is a pity that she was not permitted to kilt her green kirtle as bravely as the original Lady Janet for whom the minister did not, after all, baptise her. Her muscles and her brains were perfectly capable of development; she should have lived in Scotland until she was sixteen and then been packed off to Oxford with her brothers, Jock and Jem; perhaps she might have struck the authorities as looking rather like a pretty girl in boy's clothes, but that, being precisely the way in which her brothers struck them, would not have mattered very much. In spite of their names, Jock and Jem were thoroughly Cleverly-Nevilles. Their mother adored them, and their father teased them and felt like a brute when their blue eyes blinked at him in polite protest. Jennifer was his favourite; he liked to see his own falcon eyes burning in her small pink and white face, and he knew instinctively that she was neither a fool nor a coward, only egregiously lazy.

"God damn my soul, the girl's even lazier than her mother!" he would say, and then he would laugh and laugh and laugh. The boys would jump in their chairs and shrink back in alarm, but neither little Jennifer nor her mother jumped or shrank at all; they laughed too, and they were laughing at Tam-Linn. The next day, very likely, the whole family would leave for Devonshire, a full fortnight earlier than the Earl had expected. He loved the dripping rocks and spongy heather of Carterhaugh with a fierce intensity, and yet when he reached Cleverly-Neville on Christmas Eve, and kissed his wife and daughter again, he was so wild with joy at the sight of them that he could very nearly, as he himself put it, have eaten them both up like a nice little pat of butter and nice little pot of cream.

Thus Jennifer Lorn was brought up within sight of a warm, pearl-colored sea, in a garden where the roses bloomed all winter if they had a bit of south wall to hold the sun behind them, and where the lilacs and laburnum came out so ridiculously early that your mind was never quite made up to look for them, and they carried a slight air of miracles about them every spring. She was brought up to eat bread and butter, and milk and honey, and rice pudding, and strawberry jam for a treat. She was brought up to wear frocks of fine India muslin and to tie blue ribbons about her waist; to go to church and sing hymns out of a velvet hymnal with a gilt cross on it; to sit on a green silk chair while her maid brushed her curls to splendour; to sit on a white bench and read Percy's Reliques; to lean over a sundial on a summer's day and wonder drowsily why she loved cream-coloured roses better than yellow ones, and why she had ever been born. This is the way in which she had been brought up, and this is the way she looked; it is easy to understand why Gerald uttered a choking cry and sprang violently to his feet when he first saw her in July, 1772, falling asleep at six o'clock on a golden-cloudy afternoon, with her red ringlets heaped like a little fire above the circle of stone.

She was precisely what he had been searching for ever since his return to England; she had been in his mind's eye all the time, correct in every detail with the possible exception of the red hair; he had imagined that her hair would be ash-blonde or pale chestnut. But that was natural enough; such a complexion had never been seen before save in combination with the fairest of flaxen tresses. He had not made the mistake of supposing that she would have blue eyes; these eyes, the colour of a thunder-storm streaked with yellow lightning, had blazed for an instant into his before the lazy eyelids covered them up, and he had known them for the most beautiful eyes in the world; he had always intended that his wife should have such eyes. He fell back rather limply against the Chinese brocade; the girl was almost too perfect. "Pretty little thing, isn't she?" Dick asked complacently. Gerald stared at him in silent disdain.

When Tam-Linn came back with the Elzevir Cicero, Gerald drew him aside. "Lord Tam-Linn," he said in a quiet, admirably-controlled voice, "I should like to ask for your permission to marry your daughter." Tam-Linn, who had thought that Gerald was going to attempt to buy the Cicero from him, was very much relieved. He had been surprised and embarrassed by the prospect of having to refuse his young friend's request; this was another matter. It never occurred to him for an instant that Gerald had seen Jennifer for the first time just five minutes ago; he took it for granted that the acquaintance was of reasonable standing, and he knew that Gerald's own standing was rather more than that.

To tell the truth, Tam-Linn did not entirely realise his daughter's astonishing beauty; he admired plump dark-haired women, of the type of his own Clarinda. Privately he thought his child had a slightly starved and eccentric air; he gave her a great many buttered scones and girdle-cakes whenever he had the opportunity, and loved the poor girl none the less for her pathetic appearance, but of course it made a difference to him in his estimate of her matrimonial chances. As for her hair, the Black Tam-Linns had always been the handsome ones; they had square impassive faces bearing the unmistakable stamp of the blood of those southerners who once built a wall across Scotland; their cleft chins and calm brown eyes were still classic. The Earl knew what it was to be called Red by cousins who looked like Roman consuls. It always gave him a shock to see Jennifer standing knee-deep in purple-red heather with her copper-red hair streaming out against a hot blue August haze; when the high wind lifted the tangled locks and bent the heather, whistling all the while like a mad thing, he thought of witches. It comforted him to remember that the lassie would soon be old enough to wear a decent snood and a sprinkling of powder.

Therefore, it is only natural that when Gerald asked Tam-Linn for his daughter's hand, the Earl made no objection, merely remarking that he would have to ask his wife, but that for his own part he would be thoroughly pleased to see his girl the daughter-in-law of his old friend Camphile.

As a matter of fact, Lord Camphile and he had never liked each other; still, it seemed the simplest thing to say under the circumstances, and in a rush of relief about the Elzevir, he said it with much geniality, reflecting meanwhile that he thanked his God that the real decision lay in Clarinda's province.

"Then may I have the privilege of a word with Lady Tam-Linn?" asked Gerald urbanely, but with a slight emphasis on the "Lady" which would have annoyed the Earl very much had he not been far too absent-minded to notice it, and which caused Dick to quiver with joy and fear. Dick's head was swimming, but on the whole he felt great pride in his youthful kinsman; in addition to this he was conscious of a pleasing sense of triumph; he had not forgotten how haughtily Gerald had stalked from the breakfast room that morning at the mention of Jennifer's name, and he debated within himself as to the advisability of rallying the dear boy upon the subject. Just as he had reached the conclusion that after dinner was always the best time, Lady Tam-Linn appeared in the doorway.

She was a very pretty little woman, much younger than her husband; her dark hair, silvered only by its sprinkling of powder, grew into a peak on her forehead; the mingled rose and dove-colour of her dress set off her fine complexion to advantage; her small feet were almost concealed by the shining buckles on her shoes. Only her lively and satirical blue eyes made her other than the charming wax doll whom Tam-Linn had longed to set above the incongruous savagery of Carterhaugh. He had fondly believed that because a woman had pink cheeks and plump white hands she must of necessity be pliant and docile; Clarinda was neither of these things. Under her lazy amiability she was both wilful and obstinate, but as her strongest desire in life was to make her husband and children happy, no great harm was done; she always encompassed her desire in her own way, and they soon learned to be satisfied with the sort of happiness she considered good for them, knowing very well that any other sort was simply out of the question. They were an exceptionally united family.

"My love," said Tam-Linn, "Mr. Poynyard wants to marry Jennifer."

His wife inspected Gerald closely before replying; she was still far too romantic to tolerate the thought of a mere marriage of convenience for her daughter. Lady Tam-Linn liked tall fair-haired men; she found Gerald's appearance most satisfactory, and considered his nose a mark of race, which indeed it was. His commanding presence and air of impassive and polite contempt impressed her; in a word, she thought him magnificent. She was not sufficiently vulgar-minded to allow the idea of his wealth to obtrude into her upper consciousness, but an aureate background swam behind him, throwing into cold and clear-edged relief the sharp lines of his figure, clad in metallic grey, with shimmering buttons on a coat the colour of steel.

His chill eyes compelled her; she was won in a moment. Gerald realised his conquest as he followed her into the Blue Parlour, but his taste was too perfect to permit of strutting; he went gravely and decorously behind her without so much as a glance in Dick's direction; his slight bow to Tam-Linn was a masterpiece of dignity and reserve.

CHAPTER TEN

From *The Venetian Glass Nephew*

New York: George H. Doran Company, 1925
London: William Heinemann, 1925
Collected Prose of Elinor Wylie. New York: Alfred A. Knopf, 1933
The Borzoi Reader. Garden City, New York: Garden City Publishing Co., 1938
Reprint; Chicago: Academy Chicago, 1984

Book One: Peter Innocent

I. Blue Balloon

Peter Innocent Bon was about to return to the Republic of Venice; although he had that very day entered upon the eighty-first year of his age, his eyes, blue as veronica flowers, were even now full of a child's tears. His heart was lighter than a flower; indeed, it danced so high and airily, and teased the tenuous cord of his mortality with such persistent malice, that he conceived of it as a toy balloon, an azure plaything in a pantomime, caught by a thread of gold to stable earth, and germane to the sky.

It will be necessary to explain to minds versed in such matters that Peter Innocent Bon must by no means be confounded with John Bona of Mondovi, a misapprehension imaginable in the ignorant, since both were cardinals and both distinguished scholars. But wider far than the mere century of time separating the lives of these holy men is the gulph that sunders their natures and their activities. Consanguinity there may have been, in reason, but the two were never spiritually akin. Peter Innocent undoubtedly possessed the Antwerp edition of his cousin's works, published in 1777, and the devotional treatise "De Sacrificio Missæ" was often in his hands; a few marginal notes attest to application saddened by bewilderment. To those desiring to achieve a better comprehension of the character of Peter Innocent Bon, cardinal priest and cardinal prefect of the Congregation of the Propaganda, the historian recommends a careful study of his poetical writings (Venice, 1790) and his notes upon liturgical subjects (Parma, 1794). His memoirs, surveying as they did almost the entire length of the eighteenth century with a bland and illuminative eye, must have contained matter of the highest interest; this valuable document was unfortunately destroyed by Madame de Staël in a passing fit of temper during the composition of "Corinne," merely because it contained a simple unadorned account of the coronation of Corilla Olimpica.

On this eighth of May, 1782, Peter Innocent, clad in the grey-brown garb of the Franciscan Friars Minor, stood dreaming among delicate grotesques in the porch of his titulary church of St. Bonaventura. It was evening; the Roman sun had lost its imperial savagery, and tempered light lay tenderly upon the cardinal's brow. His face, that had beheld the secular world for eighty years, was lifted to the more transparent heaven; forgetting Rome and even the Vatican, he regarded the Holy City above the horns of the new moon. He looked affectionately yet familiarly into the little loopholes of the stars, with none of the bitter hunger of the returning exile; to Peter Innocent the bread of earth was never salty, nor the stairs of heaven too steep. As a boy may see at evening the lighted windows of his mother's kitchen, he saw without surprise celestial preparation for his home-coming through a bright chink that may have been Aldebaran. Tugging at its gilded thread, his heart danced over him, a blue balloon in deeper aërial blue.

Above the chiselled silver of his head, his heart danced, expanded by happiness and an exquisite gratitude towards all humanity and the Son of God made man. In particular, his heart blessed the new pope, Pius VI, for although Giovanni Angelo Braschi had ruled Christendom for some seven years, Peter Innocent never thought of him save as a handsome innovation, superseding with the suavest courtesy the cardinal's dead patron and beloved friend, the Franciscan Clement XIV. Now this same Pius, whom Peter Innocent a little feared, the more that he was beautiful and brilliant and vain, proposed for reasons of his own to visit the green lagoons and golden palaces of Venice, having among his suite, again for reasons of his own, Peter Innocent Bon, cardinal prefect of the Congregation of the Propaganda.

The cardinal did not concern himself with reasons; he thought of Venice, and the bright thread pulled hard upon his heart. He had not seen that city for nearly thirty years; not since his brother Nicholas Bon was banished to the monastery of Venda by the Council of Ten and Inquisitors of the Holy Office. In that same year Paul Dona was confined in the fortress of Palma, and five years later the noble Angelo Querini was imprisoned in the castle of St. Felice at Verona.

For a time the spirit of Peter Innocent suffered a faint infusion of bitterness throughout its milk and honey; he began to believe in spies and politics, and found himself disliking the Dominicans without feeling any particular love for the Jesuits. But he managed with admirable tact to hold himself aloof from all dissension, and it is certain that his veined patrician hand was not among those which upheld the fainting resolution of Lorenzo Ganganelli as the pontiff traced the momentous syllables of the brief, *Dominus ac redemptor,* and signed it Clement, servant of the servants of God.

But this was years, and happy years, ago, and to-day Peter Innocent could remember that all these brave and liberal senators had been set free either by death or by the reforms of '63, and that Querini had travelled in Switzerland and become a valued friend of Voltaire's. The cardinal had long ago forgiven Venice, and upon this Ascension Eve his heart was a blue balloon because it was going home.

He thought of himself as a child upon other Ascension eves and morrows, in a past not dim at all, but radiant as a double dawn in sky and water. He saw the *Bucintoro* setting forth from Santa Lucia, a gilded barge arrayed in cloth of gold, with winged lions, tritons, nereids, painted with gold and burnished by the sun, with the great standard of the republic crackling like lightning overhead. He thought of the ancient glory of Venice, and of the Lion of the Evangelist. His grey habit of the Seraphic Order fell from his shoulders, and he was a child again, in a coat of sapphire velvet, with a silver feather in his cap.

Softly, very softly, the supple folds of dun-colour descended once more over this remembered magnificence, and Peter Innocent felt the worn, warm fabric about his fragile bones. Here, too, was cause for gratitude, for the new pope had permitted him to continue in this ingenuous disguise, first granted him by the generosity of Clement, so that he alone of the pontifical family went comfortably impoverished, clad in the mystic tatters of Assisi. Within a remote wing of the Vatican a wardrobe of ebony and figured brass guarded vestments of white and red and green, of violet and black and the more curious sheen of metal, with robes and rochets of a less sacral character and rich liturgical gloves and stockings, intermixed with honorific decorations.

Peter Innocent loved best to drift, elusive as a skeleton leaf, along the streets of Rome, recognized by all, but accosted by none save an occasional German traveller or English milord; the legerity of the French mind made the Gallic visitor quick to comprehend his desire for solitude, and the very transparency of the masking rendered it invulnerable. Whether or not he believed himself effectively disguised remained a mystery to the last. He spoke but little; indeed it was a common saying at the time that Clement had forgotten to unseal his mouth; his smile, however, impressed even the most impious as a small flame burning perpetually within the silver shadow of his countenance.

At the conclusion of Vespers, he often knelt in a sculptured recess of the Church of St. Bonaventura, while the words *O salutaris hostia* were borne upon the wings of ancient music towards the benediction. As the priest, his shoulders wrapped in the humeral veil, lifted the monstrance from the lighted altar and with it described in that already consecrated air the sign of the cross, the tears of Peter Innocent aspersed like holy water whatever evil might survive within those walls, beneath that vaulted nave.

4. Crystal Monsters

Blue dusk, thicker than fog and tinted with expressed essence of heaven along the falling colour of the dew, enveloped Peter Innocent as he slipped from the lighted doorway of the Incurabili; the music prolonged itself through other channels than his ears, and seemed to influence the hue of the most distant star and the perfume of the nearest pomegranate flower. He was happy, but a little loneliness, even a little fear, tinctured his mood. He had been unable to identify either of his old friends, and had found himself too shy to ask for them among the brocaded crowd of notables. Unobserved, he had sought the consolation of the twilight; he loved to be alone, but to-night his tranquillity had somehow failed him. He felt cold and rather tremulous as a touch fell upon his shoulder.

It was Alvise Luna, the glass-blower of Murano. He had grown very old, and his pale eyes were sunken in a face blank and dusty as a bag of yellow meal. Peter Innocent was shocked by the man's appearance, and greeted him sympathetically.

"Eminence," said Luna in a voice threaded by a whine, "I had not hoped to be recognized, nor, if recognized, acknowledged as an acquaintance by your Eminence. I have fallen upon evil times. I, whose ancestors worked in crystal for the great Duke of Buckingham and visited Tuscany at the invitation of the munificent Cosimo Second, I have not, to be frank with you, one copper coin wherewith to brighten another, I have drunk water for a fortnight, and the things I have eaten are not fit to be mentioned in your eminent presence. I am reduced to working for the infamous Giorgio Barbaria, who wishes to manufacture black glass bottles on the English lines; I have, as you may remember, considerable knowledge of foreign factories, and he pays me a dog's wages to instruct him. I am starving; my wife and children are starving; my little grandchildren are already dead from malnutrition. May I humbly beg your Eminence to aid me in my undeserved and dreadful trouble?"

This Luna was a liar and a sorcerer, and the Holy Office was already upon his path, which led through some of the most unsavoury cellars of Venice, marked out by a slimy brilliance like the track of a snail. But Peter Innocent did not know this, and had he known, he would not have understood it. He saw that the man was frightened, and he believed that he was hungry. As a matter of fact, Luna had plenty of money and merely wanted more; at the moment an enormous supper of polenta was distending his greasy waistcoat. But he was a dyspeptic, and his wry neck and hollow eyes looked wretched enough to move a more obdurate heart than Peter Innocent's.

"Of course," said the gentle old man, "of course, my poor friend, I will do what I can to help you."

An hour later, Peter Innocent was picking his slow, uncertain way down a damp and noisome corridor; Luna followed him, holding a candle as high as the dripping ceiling would permit. They descended a worn flight of stone stairs, and found themselves in a low-vaulted chamber whose debased Byzantine arches were dimly illuminated by a pair of ship's lanterns dependent therefrom.

This apartment was but too evidently a cellar, for a good three inches of water, cold and ambiguous, polluted the embroidered clocks upon the cardinal's stockings. Nevertheless, certain portions of the walls were covered by tapestries smouldering with the rich fancies of the Renaissance, and a number of carved cabinets and tables showed surfaces inlaid with brass or panelled in exotic lacquer. At one end of the chamber's secretive length, a small furnace filled with wood ashes made a spot of expiring rose-amber in the gloom.

Luna walked to the centre of the room, and, rapidly waving his guttering tallow back and forth, ignited in a flash a score of white wax candles cupped in coloured glass. Peter Innocent saw that a superb chandelier hung from the highest vaulting of the roof, a fantastic thing of flowers and icicles and silver bells, tinkling in the midst of squalor. And now, with a tinted radiance flooding every corner of the cobwebbed cellar, a hundred graceful and preposterous shapes sprang into the enchanted view: winged and maned and dolphin-finned, griffins and lions, stags and peacocks, and monsters fabulously horned and taloned.

The cardinal perceived in addition to these savage and exquisite creatures the accustomed implements of the glass-blower's trade: pontils and blowpipes, pincers and wooden battledores. Upon a platform, raised above the pervasive dampness of the stone-flagged floor, stood the workman's chair, with its rigid parallel arms suggesting some rude instrument of torture. Seated within this strange machine was a mysterious stranger, wrapped in a black cloak, and wearing a small mask of black velvet.

Peter Innocent at once became aware of an element of masquerade in the appearance of this person. Having himself long ago assumed a disguise, albeit an holy one, he readily observed the same quality in the dress of others, and as readily ascribed it to the most innocuous desire for privacy. He took the gentleman to be a person of simple and retiring disposition, and acknowledged courteously and at once Luna's gesture of introduction. The stranger rose, displaying an impressive figure, tall and muscular. He wore a quantity of beautiful lace, and his rings were diamonds of the first brilliance; save for these elegant details, his clothes were of a uniform sable hue. His head was covered by a short chestnut peruke, and through the slits of his mask his eyes glinted very dark and bright. The skin of his face and hands was swarthy and faintly lined; the cardinal judged him to be past his first youth.

"Your Eminence," said Luna in French, which he spoke fluently, having, for several disgraceful reasons, been much in Paris, "permit me to present M. de Chastelneuf, Chevalier de Langeist." The latter title was pronounced in the German manner, and the cardinal was at a loss to conjecture the stranger's nationality until he spoke. His manners were courtly, if a little antiquated and florid, but he conversed with a strong Venetian accent, and Peter Innocent had no doubt that he was a native of the republic.

The chevalier kissed the cardinal's hand with immense politeness, and began at once to speak of the prelate's poetical works, displaying a quite remarkable knowledge and acumen. In this way, and through the use of copious quotation from the classics, the gentleman contrived to convey an impression of learning and respectability, and Peter Innocent felt sure he must be a person of consequence.

Such, in a measure, was indeed the case, for M. de Chastelneuf, as this narrative must continue to call him, had at one time or another attracted the attention of almost every court of Europe, and on this very evening no less a notable than Messer Grand himself had given our gentleman much good advice not unconnected with the miasmic quality of the Venetian air, and the superior salubriety of Munich or Vienna. And since it was the chevalier's invariable habit to travel in a superb English carriage, emblazoned with the arms of a ruined lord, and as, moreover, he seldom travelled alone, he had been faced with the disagreeable necessity of selling his diamonds and his point d'Alençon without delay. Save for the fortunate intervention of Luna, who knew the cardinal's simplicity was good for at least a thousand sequins, M. de Chastelneuf might have been forced to part with his cross of the Order of the Gold Spur. It is not surprising that his happiness in greeting Peter Innocent was unfeigned and infectious.

Presently the cardinal found himself ensconced within the glass-blower's misshapen armchair, with dry slippers upon his feet, and a couple of hot bricks under these. A glass of excellent Levantine Muscat warmed his vitals; the long room appeared less cavernous, and the crystal apparitions which filled it glowed like jewels in the renewed stream of his own vivacity. His two companions were persons of wit and esoteric learning, and his admiration for Luna increased as he examined one by one the marvellous progeny of the workman's art. As for the chevalier, the delicacy of his mind was equalled only by its ascetic and fastidious grace: Peter Innocent was soothed and enraptured by this refined society.

The chevalier removed his mask, and his face showed handsome and aquiline, almost Oriental in its dusky tints, yet all Venetian in the liveliness and valour which informed its every smile. He had a nose like a falcon, and his deep-set eyes were black and gold. He told Peter Innocent that he had, in his youth, been honoured by the friendship of Benedict XIV, who had once taken his advice upon some little matters of no importance.

Suddenly M. de Chastelneuf rose to his very considerable height, at the same time making, for the benefit of Luna's eyes alone, an enigmatical sign whose nature it is impossible to describe. Luna also rose; the pair appeared to move in unison to some unheard and rhythmical injunction; salt and spices were destroyed upon the fire, and their smoke permitted to dim the purer radiance of the candle-flames. Then at an unintelligible word pronounced by the altered voice of Chastelneuf, the incredible came to pass.

Peter Innocent beheld a golden griffin lift his wings to fan the air; a stag, of azure glass dappled with the same gold, stepped with a fairy pride across the expanse of Chinese lacquer which separated him from his mate, and the two, meeting, caressed each other with delicate gestures of affection. A humming-bird, with feathers blown in pearl-colour and crimson, flew from his perch, alighting on the leafy chandelier; the spray that received him bent and swayed, and from its largest rose a petal drifted to the floor.

There is not the slightest use in pretending that Peter Innocent was shocked or even very greatly surprised. His mind moved happily in an atmosphere of miracles, and the charming nature of these phenomena precluded any suspicion of evil. He felt like a child who perceives at his first carnival a blue sky flowering with confetti, or who is presented at Christmas-time with one of those delightful German toys call Christbaum, bright with silver foil and tiny scarlet candles. So, without uncomfortable amazement, he stared enchanted at the delicious marvel of awakened life.

CHAPTER ELEVEN

From *The Orphan Angel*

New York: Alfred A. Knopf, 1926
London: William Heinemann, 1927 (published as *Mortal Image*)
Collected Prose of Elinor Wylie. New York: Alfred A. Knopf, 1933
Reprint; New York: Popular Library, no date.

I. Western Wave

On the eighth of July, 1822, at half past six in the evening, the American clipper-built brig *Witch of the West* was beating out of Leghorn Harbour, close-hauled upon the increasing wind. She was a smart little vessel; beneath the varnished black of immaculate paint a new copper bottom glittered bravely as she leaned over nearly upon her beam-ends in the racing glass-green sea.

In place of the dried codfish, furs, and Virginian tobacco with which she had put forth from Boston seven weeks before, the pretty ship now carried a luxurious cargo of wine, olive oil, and candied tropic fruits; her shining surfaces and slender compact proportions concealed an appropriate core of honeyed essences and spice. Yet, as she struggled under naked and singing shrouds against the force and violence of the summer hurricane, she wore an air no less valiant than graceful, like the aërial composure of a cloud.

"If we spin her round upon her heel, as we oughter, and put back to port, you'll hang, Davy, or I'll eat my oilskins," said the skipper, a red-haired Yankee from New Bedford; he spat an impatient expletive and a thin stream of tobacco juice within an inch of young David Butternut's excellent sea-boots. The captain had shipped upon an old-fashioned whaler, in the capacity of cabin-boy, during the most formative period of his youth; his manners were often rough to the point of boorishness, but a soft heart beat under the horny tarpaulin of his seaman's coat.

"You'll hang, I calculate," repeated the skipper pessimistically. "And mebbe you'll burn too, for you boys picked the quarrel in the porch of a church, and that's what these Eyetalians call sacrilegious, I reckon. You've attracted the notice of the authorities, and I doubt that I'd have power to help you, my lad. We got our clearance papers just in time to save your skin, otherwise I'd never have sailed into the jaws of this dirty weather."

"I know it, sir," replied the youth with becoming modesty, "and trust me, Cap'n, to be properly grateful." David Butternut was a tall muscular stripling from the coasts of Maine; the changing fortunes which had uprooted him from a forest to set him upon the slanting deck of a brig appeared to have fitted him into his surroundings as neatly as any shipbuilder transplants a pine-tree to carry spread of sail. "Not that I'd have you drown the other boys along of me; I don't see as there's such an almighty difference betwixt hanging and drowning, after all. Go back if you've a mind to, sir, and don't never bother about me; I'm not worthy of any such kindness, and I don't rightly know as I'd rather not hang; it's a fine dry death, when everything's said and done."

"No, no, Dave my boy, you're wrong there," the captain insisted with an indulgent smile, "as you'd realize full well if ever you'd been strung from the yard-arm, like I was once in the good old days. Cut down in the nick of time, by the special intercession of the first mate, but my throat was sore for a week, I do assure you. No, it's a damned uncomfortable death, lad, and I hope it's not necessary that you should hang this voyage. Jasper Cross was a nasty customer, for all his pleasant gentlemanly airs, and there's some of us as knows you only acted in self-defence; yet the law's a pretty crank thing to handle, and I'd not give a wooden dollar as the price of your neck in Leghorn tonight."

David shot an appreciative glance towards the captain, in whom he had long recognised a true if an untender friend. "Thank you kindly, sir, I'm sure," he whispered huskily, brushing the sleeve of his pea-jacket across his ingenuous blue eyes.

"Now, boy," said the captain in a brisk business-like manner, "seeing as you've left us kinder short-handed with that there fist of yours, mebbe you'd better attend to reefing the topsail, and quit worrying about murders."

Butternut turned cheerfully enough to this change of employment, and good Captain Ffoulkastle remained for a moment lost in reverie, gazing out over the tumultuous sea, where all the elements of sublimity and terror raged unseen behind a descending veil of darkness.

Suddenly, with the amazement of a thunderclap, he beheld a human countenance emerge from this sinister obscurity to float upon the dark like a drowning star, without mortality or substance.

"Man overboard!" cried Captain Ffoulkastle in a tremendous voice; he spoke to himself in an awe-struck murmur. "Strike my timbers if I didn't think it was that sarpent Jasper, come aboard to pester us, but here's Jasper's corpse still a-rolling in the bloody scuppers, lads not having time to tidy up along of this blasted storm. Still, I'll stake my soul it's Jasper's ghost I seen . . . " whispered the captain nervously. Another great wave lifted the mysterious face well-nigh to the level of the vessel's plunging side, where it shone brighter and whiter than before in a flash from the larboard lantern.

"Man overboard!" shouted the captain a second time, and in response to his call young David Butternut leaped from the mast as from the summit of a swaying forest tree and sprang into the blackness of the ocean.

"Didn't even wait to kick off them heavy boots of his," observed the captain philosophically. "Well, there goes another of my able seamen!" Aloud he bellowed "Ready about!" and "Helms down!" and was about to add "Lower the boat!" when he perceived that David, by some miracle of superhuman strength and agility, and by the material aid of a rope flung by his affectionate comrades, had indeed regained the deck, bearing in his arms a singular and unearthly burden.

"It's Jasper's attendant angel!" breathed the captain, surprised into a momentary pang of pure mysticism.

The scene was solemn to the extremity of awe; upon the deck, illuminated by the faint glimmer of a lantern, lay the blood-stained corpse of Jasper Cross, and above this tragic indication of impermanence appeared, supported in the arms of David Butternut, a veritable image of the same figure, but brighter, clearer, fairer, as if from the blessing of another planet. The creature's eyes were closed, but its countenance wore a look of beatitude and innocence infinitely touching to behold, and the composure of the brow was childlike and serene.

"Cap'n, I don't know what I've snatched from the fury of the waters," said David simply, "but I do know this: it's something good and something beautiful, and if I've preserved its body from destruction, I think it's saved my soul from everlasting death!"

In his own face was mirrored a reflection of the preternatural light shining upon the stranger's forehead, and as he gazed from one to the other of these curious visions, this the secular portent of mortality, and that the embodiment of spiritual grace, he trembled and wept as if he had that moment come naked into a legendary world.

"Give Davy a tot of rum," said the captain compassionately. "The poor boy must be chilled to the bone. And some of you lazy lubbers look to the stranger and see whether there's any life mixed with the sea-water in his innards."

Captain Ffoulkastle had satisfied himself that the unknown was a human creature, and as such singularly innocuous, but to the superstitious sailors he was still an object of fear; not until the blustering second mate had led the way with a laugh and a brutal jest did any dare to lay his hand upon the body, now lying tranquilly along the blood-stained deck.

"Our Jasper's twin, by the pretty face on him," cried the mate with a coarse chuckle. "And both of them deader nor doornails, damn their silly eyes; we won't pour good Demerara after stinking sea-water down the throats of no drowned men, will we, boys?"

He was about to spurn the motionless form with the toe of his great tarry boot, but David Butternut sprang forward in time to prevent this act of cruelty, and the indignant murmurs of the men soon warned the mate that such sentiments were unsuited to the hour and the grave occasion. Swallowing a curse, he applied himself with tolerable interest to the problem of ascertaining whether or no life yet lingered in the stranger's breast.

“Gone, I do declare,” said the mate casually, dropping the cold hand and shrugging his shoulders. “Well, reckon there’s nothing to do but pitch him back into that pesky tea-cup where he come from.”

“But, by graminy,” cried David in horror, “we’re a-going to try to bring him round, ain’t we? I know in my heart he’s some kind of messenger from God, and if we reject him now, indifferent-like, what’s to become of us all? I asks you honest, is that the face of an angel, or ain’t it?” None cared to contradict him; without another word he unscrewed the flask of rum which the captain had given him and attempted to pour a few drops of the fiery liquid between the colourless lips of the unconscious stranger.

Presently the captain’s repeated cry of “All hands ahoy!” left the young sailor the sole occupant of that retired portion of the deck, but still David knelt devoutly beside the mysterious visitant, forgetful of the storm and its attendant pandemonium, and searching with an agonized attention the peaceful face of the unknown.

Meanwhile his mind was full of confused prayers and images, in which the continued life of this mortal, snatched by his strength from the blackness of annihilation, seemed the dear embodiment of something lost and infinitely cherished.

“To make up for Jasper!” he muttered to himself with a shaking mouth, “oh, to make up for Jasper! Please, please, come back, and I shall be forgiven!”

2

As if in answer to David’s low entreaty, the stranger stirred, and, opening large blue eyes, gazed with an expression of innocent bewilderment straight into the small blue eyes of his preserver.

With a cry of joy, David caught the living creature’s hand in a strong salty grasp, and, to his own and the other’s extreme amazement, covered the cold wet fingers with religious kisses.

“Thank God!” he cried, while the tears mingled with the bitter spray upon his cheeks. “Thank God you’ve come back! Now everything will be all right, I reckon; I thanks you with all my heart for coming, and I bless you for ever and ever.”

“Where am I?” asked the stranger in a very faint voice; his voice seemed to travel from tragic distances, and yet he was smiling a little at David’s vehemence. “And where is Edward, and what has become of that poor boy, Charles Vivian the sailor?”

“I am that poor boy David Butternut, a sailor and a murderer,” declared David with fierce humility. Leastways, I reckon as I’m a murderer, though not going for to do more than bust his head for him when he ups and draws a knife on me. But I've a goldarned heavy hand, more's the pity, and there he lays as cold as so many pounds of salt cod, and 'twas me as killed him, and I won't deny it; no, never to you, whatever tale I tells the police when we land in Boston. Can you be friends with a murderer, young fellow? Cause I want for you to be my friend, and yet I'm a terrible sinner to ask for friendship from the likes of you."

"The likes of me!" repeated the stranger softly and ironically. "The likes of me will not refuse your friendship, David Butternut, nor fear to shake the hand which all unwittingly has sent another man to unravel the ultimate enigma of the grave." He essayed weakly to offer his own right hand to David, who took it with a cry of gratitude.

"You know I was so lucky as to save your life, don't you?" asked David a moment later with renewed cheerfulness. "Yes, stranger, I hopped into that there dirty old sea, and I pulled you out as easy as rolling off a log in the Kennebec. But now tell me, seeing as we're friends, are you an angel or a man, and are you any kin to Jasper there? for you're alike as two peas, only he's a rotten black pea and you're a brand-new silver one. Who are you, young feller, and what might be your name, and do you happen to come from heaven or anywhere along those coasts?"

"No, not precisely," answered the stranger gently and a little sadly. "I do not come from anywhere along those coasts, nor am I any kin to Jasper there, save as all men are brothers. As for my name, it is . . . "

But here the stranger's voice failed him so completely that David Butternut, bending low, could with difficulty distinguish any sound, and that perplexing and dispersed upon the wind. At the same time he noticed with alarm that the other's countenance had assumed an excessive and sorrowful pallor, and that his large blue eyes were closed as if in sleep.

"Are you all right?" he inquired sharply, a chilly sensation contracting his heart almost to suffocation. "Hey, there, young feller, are you all right, or are you a-going to die after all?" And he shook the other by his thin shoulder, as one who rouses an obstinate and beloved dreamer from oblivion.

A slight smile was discernible upon the stranger's pale and composed lips, and he contrived to enunciate, slowly, but with exquisite politeness, a few words of amused reassurance.

"I am exceedingly sorry to constitute myself a nuisance, and I would not for the world have you distress yourself upon my poor account, but I believe, my dear David that I am about to solve the great mystery of dissolution."

Apparently suiting the action to the word, he lay relaxed and motionless upon the deck, while David, with a loud cry of dismay, ran headlong towards the lighted cabin.

The captain, in dripping tarpaulins and very high boots, was filling his pipe by the fitful illumination of a brazen lamp suspended from the ceiling by chains and shaken violently by the motion of the ship. Under the falling alternations of flame and shadow his weatherbeaten face was intent and tranquil.

"Well, what is it now?" he called testily, in response to David's frantic knock and immediate entrance. "I calculate those lazy dogs are skeered of this capful of wind, and want me to sing them to sleep. But who in hell told you to come in here?" he demanded irascibly, recognising his visitor.

"Oh, please, sir," David began in agitated accents, "that there young stranger has been and died again on deck, and I want for you to come along and look at him, and mebbe give him just a drop of that special peach brandy that we had on the Fourth of July. Aw, Cap'n, I'd be that grateful if you'd spare him just a little drop!"

"Come, come, Dave my lad," said the captain calmly presenting to these agonised entreaties the impassive front of a carven storm-scarred fragment of hickory wood, "keep cool and I'll spare you a minute for this business, though it's sheer waste of time fussing over a dead boy with all you kicking live ones on my hands. It's the time and not the brandy that I grudge him, Dave, but it's worth it if we can bring him round and put him in the starboard watch to take Jasper's place. And that reminds me," said the captain indulgently, his eyes on David's simple honest countenance, "I have a fine scheme for saving your precious neck, my lad, when we land in Boston."

David paid no heed to his remarks, watching instead with the most fascinated attention the decanting of a minute quantity of peach brandy into a thick blue tea-cup, which feat the captain performed with amazing delicacy and skill. Without another word the two sturdy sailors made their way through unnoticed prodigies of wind and thunder to that part of the ship where the mysterious stranger lay entranced or dead.

To the captain, and in a far greater degree to David, there appeared something obscurely moving and magical in the scene now presented to their view. The ultimate curtain of the sky was split at intervals by hieroglyphs of lightning and the immense profundities of cloud seemed audible in thunder. Above their heads, the rigging of the ship was plucked to an intense thin music by the hurricane, and driven sheets of green and silver water drowned them in cold and phosphorescent brilliance.

Upon the slanting deck two figures were disposed, miraculously still in the midst of this delirium. Jasper, with the bruise darkening at his temple and blood upon his brow, stared upward with an angry questioning insistence, but the other lay as if asleep, with quiet eyelids and dark hair drenched with spray, and the locks of hair were folded about his forehead like a spiked and ghostly crown.

3

"They both look just about equally dead as drowned rats," said the captain, shaking off the atmosphere of supernatural awe with an impatient movement of his massive shoulders. "But I reckon as this one can be revived with a little judicious encouragement, and a mite of creature comfort. Then," said the captain briskly, for he was after all an eminently practical man, "you'll be safe as a landlocked harbour, according to this plan of mine. Once get this fellow on his sea-legs, and slushing down the main-mast from the royal-mast-head," said the captain with anticipatory gusto, "and you won't be able to tell him from Jasper, and no more will the Boston police, or my name ain't Abner Ffoulkastle!" And he gave David a hearty punch in the ribs before kneeling down, with becoming gravity, to feel the stranger's pulse and to force between his lips the entire contents of the thick blue tea-cup.

"There's life in the young dog yet," he informed David, who waited breathless in an agony of fear. "Yes, he'll be hauling at a hawser by to-morrow morning, with his ribs lined with good salt beef and sea-bread. Now Dave, I want you to understand that it's all to your profit to learn him the ropes, as they say, and make a useful sailor out of him, for by this means you'll save yourself from the gallows and the other boys from a deal of extry work. Do you catch on, my lad?"

"Yes, sir; I think so, sir," murmured David in confusion. "You want for me to learn this stranger to take Jasper's place on shipboard. . . . "

"Yes, and on shore too, when the time comes," said the captain with a kindly chuckle. "Jasper was an orphan and black sheep, from some God-forsaken high-and-dry hole out west, and I hardly look for much trouble from his relatives. If we can satisfy the port authorities in Boston that we come home with the same crew that we shipped on sailing, that'll be enough for your purposes. Your mates won't split on you, and as for this young fellow, he seems by his face to be a gentle obliging sort of chap, and one that would be glad enough to help a friend in a little emergency. Wouldn't you, my lad? He added, with a smile at the unknown, who at this moment opened his eyes and gazed inquiringly about him.

"I shall be most happy to help my friend David by any honourable act which lies within my powers to perform," he answered at once, in a firm if somewhat far-away voice, with a quick surprising flash of blue from his large intelligent eyes. At the same time he essayed to rise, but the captain thrust him down again with a brief peremptory gesture.

"No, you lay there, stranger, till we've done our little transformation act," he said cheerfully. "Here, you David, run and fetch Jasper's Sunday clothes, while I strip these wet rags off this lad and shove 'em overboard. But no—I've a brighter idee than even that—we'll rig Jasper out in the stranger's suit, and then if any body is found, by bad luck," said the captain with a jovial laugh, "they'll think it yours, mate, and nobody's likely to suspect our Davy of killing *you!*"

While David hurried below in search of Jasper's Sunday outfit, the captain busied himself in peeling from the stranger's slender limbs the cold and dripping garments which had clothed them. A pair of black pantaloons, a short black jacket, somewhat the worse for wear, a white shirt unbuttoned at the neck, and the customary quantity of underlinen completed their number, and by the time that David arrived with the necessary covering, the unknown youth lay naked and shivering in the chilly wind, protesting feebly against the captain's forcible removal of his property.

"Please be careful of the books; I do entreat you to be careful of Keats and Sophocles," he cried faintly, but the captain heeded him not at all, and proceeded calmly upon his course, stripping Jasper's body and methodically reclothing it in the short black jacket and the shabby pantaloons.

"Never saw such a pair of fools as you two boys in all my born days," he grunted contemptuously, seeing David's averted face and the stranger's wild and stag-like eyes shaded by a thin cold hand, and hearing their united murmurs of horror and surprise. "Are you scared of poor Jasper's dead corpse, David Butternut, you that had the guts to strike him down, and are you, my lad, who lately faced the raging ocean without particular signs of fear, hiding your eyes from a mere harmless murdered boy? For shame, I say to both of you; your conduct's unworthy of men and sailors. Turn to, and help me, David, for Jasper's a damned dead weight to heave over, I can tell you."

At last, and without the aid of his young companions, the captain's self-imposed duty was completed, and, lifting Jasper's corpse in his mighty arms, he carried it to the rail, and balanced it there above the turbulent and racing sea.

"My Keats, my Sophocles!" cried the stranger in an agonized whisper. "Oh, I do beg of you not to throw my Sophocles into the ocean!" His large blue eyes were full of tears.

"He means the books he has in his pockets, sir," explained David. "Leastways, they're Jasper's pockets now, I suppose, but the books belong to the stranger, and I can see he sets great store by them."

"I can't be bothered with no books!" shouted the captain with magnificent scorn. "Now, David, I'm going to shove your messmate overboard, and if you want to bid him goodbye, here's your last chance. Well, I can't stand here all night waiting for you to make up your mind, my lad; here goes, Jasper Cross, and may the Lord have mercy upon your soul!"

The body descended through the darkness into the whirling pit of the waters, and its phosphorescent track was a moment visible and then no more. The captain and David removed their caps; the stranger closed his eyes and seemed to meditate or pray.

"I could find it in my heart to desire for this poor fellow's mortal remains a more classic dignity of requiem," he said at length with some emotion. "And yet is it not, after all, singularly fitting that a sailor's clay should be thus committed to the vaulted caverns of the crystal wave? I have frequently observed . . . "

"And I have frequently observed that you young rascals talk too much," said the captain shortly. "Moreover, you're shivering fit to shake your teeth out, and if David doesn't hustle you into those dry warm clothes you'll take your death of cold. Now Davy, look alive, and let's see how this lad appears in a proper outfit. Rub him down a bit with this here bandanna, and button him up smart in them Sunday togs, and I dare say he'll be a decent enough looking chap when you've done with him."

4

The storm had by now somewhat abated, and an occasional gleam of tarnished moonlight lit the swift procession of the clouds. By this illumination, and by the rays of the larboard lantern, David Butternut noticed with compassion the stranger's pallor and evident exhaustion, and with the utmost neatness and dispatch he proceeded to clothe him in the comfortable garments from Jasper's locker, and to chafe his frozen hands into a condition distantly resembling warmth.

"When you've finished, bring him along to my cabin," called the captain, disappearing down the deck. "Get the cook to dry Jasper's old clothes in the galley, and they'll do him for every-day. I'll see that he gets a drop of hot grog from the steward, for he looks as if he needed it."

"How do you feel now, stranger?" asked David solicitously when the two found themselves alone.

"Oh, I shall do very well, I think," returned the other evasively, as if unwilling to be led into complaint. "I shall probably be none the worse for my experience, after a crust of bread and a good night's sleep. But tell, me David, was Jasper a wicked man?"

"Not what you'd really call wicked," replied David charitably. "He was a queer mixture, was Jasper, with a face like a choir-boy's, half the time, and half the time like a devil's; with beautiful manners, gentleman's manners, and no book-learning at all, savage and revengeful, in a way of speaking, and yet with a soft heart for any woman as cared to fool him; free with his money, when he had any, and a good enough friend when he was sober. But he was hardly ever sober," added David with a burst of honesty, "and he was so ignorant, stranger, if you'll credit me, that he couldn't hardly write his own name. Funny to think of your books in poor old Jasper's pockets, down there where even the great fishes ain't got no eyes!"

The stranger shuddered a little, but David went on unheeding, driven by a painful excitement into the appeasement of confession.

"'Twas his craze for women killed him in the end, you might say, though I suppose I killed him right enough with the fist of mine, only I never meant for to do it, I'll swear on a stack of Bibles–and God strike me dead if I'd lie to a friend, a kind friend like you, and you believe me, don't you, Shiloh?"

"What is that curious name by which you have just addressed me, David? asked the stranger, a look of keen intellectual curiosity lighting his wan countenance.

"Shiloh? Why Shiloh out of the scriptures, to be sure; 'twas you yourself told me to call you that just before you fainted. Then I knew for certain what I had somehow suspected all along; that you were sent by God to save me from damnation. I can't explain it, but I know your coming has made it all fair and square about Jasper, and because I raised you up out of the devouring sea I'm no longer a murderer, praise be to heaven!"

"But who was Shiloh?" persisted the unknown. "I seem to have encountered the word repeatedly during my career; Byron called me Shiloh before he called me the Snake, and I know of course that the name occurs with frequency in the Scriptures; but I retain a strong impression that Shiloh is a place rather than a person."

"Sometimes it's a place right enough," David admitted. "But don't you remember the chapter in Genesis where old Jacob is a-scolding of his sons, and almighty mean the old man is to some of them, how he says as the sceptre shall not depart from Judah until Shiloh come? That's you, stranger, I reckon, and you knew it yourself a while ago, but has most likely forgotten it on account of being cold and tired and sorrowful. Come with me now, Shiloh, my dear friend Shiloh that has saved my soul, and I will find you food and a place to sleep, and to-morrow I will teach you to be a sailor."

So saying, he very tenderly assisted the stranger to rise, and the two young men stood face to face in the intermittent moonlight, and tall and slender as twin pillars of some temple of the sea. The stranger swayed a little, but David stood strong as stone, and where the other's blowing hair was darkness shot with silver, David's was close and curly like a golden cap, and where the other was pale, David was ruddy like his namesake, and his blue eyes met the wilder, wider eyes with infinite humility and trust.

"Just about my height, you are," said David happily. "And now catch a-hold of my arm, and come along to the captain's cabin for a nice glass of hot grog."

Captain Ffoulkastle looked up with frank curiosity as the two companions knocked and entered. Without a word he waved his hand towards a locker, where they seated themselves side by side in attitudes of respectful attention and courteous patience. He handed the stranger a large glass of steaming rum punch, which the young man regarded silently and with apparent disapproval.

"Drink it up, son," said the captain in an authoritative voice. "Orders is orders aboard the *Witch of the West,* and you're ordered to drink that toddy without making any ungrateful faces. Don't be dainty, but get it under your belt double quick; now, then, down she goes with a yo-heave-ho, my hearty."

The stranger obeyed, swallowed the scalding drink with an expression of acute agony, and leaned back rather limply against the panelling, exhausted by the unnatural effort.

"Take the glass from him, Davy; I don't want it broken," said the captain. "Pour yourself a nip from that jug on the table, and then go out on deck and wait there until I call you. I've got this Jasper business to attend to with our young friend here, and perhaps it might embarrass you a bit; also he may have family affairs to discuss with me, and for that we need privacy. Run along, and don't sit there gaping like a stuck pig."

David, his eyes fixed admiringly upon the stranger's dreaming countenance, sidled slowly from the cabin, closing the door cautiously behind him, and the captain turned to his guest with a brisk and kindly question.

CHAPTER TWELVE

From *Mr. Hodge and Mr. Hazard*

New York: Alfred A. Knopf, 1928
Collected Prose of Elinor Wylie. New York: Alfred A. Knopf, 1933
Reprint; Chicago: Academy Chicago, 1984

Advertisement

The author of the following little romance begs that the reader will accept it as a work of fiction pure and simple, nor seek to discover within its pages portraits of dead or living persons. The central character may indeed be regarded as a composite miniature of the whole generation of early nineteenth century romantics, but reduced to so small a scale and depicted in colours so subdued as to render the likenesses invisible. No attempt has been made either to conceal or to emphasize the traits of the unlucky type to which Mr. Hazard belongs and whose imperfections he may serve to illustrate. He was evidently the victim of an excessive sensibility which the high order of his talents failed to stiffen into character. With gifts and natural abilities far above the common, he nevertheless lacked the power of self-discipline to a regrettable degree, and therefore fell an easy prey to morbid introspection and the disapproval of Mr. Hodge.

The author would be sorry to burden the illustrious shoulders of any genius with the hollow pack of Mr. Hazard's opinions; his eccentricities are his own, and if she has purloined a pistol ball or a black felt hat from his contemporary or hers she hopes to be forgiven. She has formed this little image of an idealist from various clays, and if, like the sculptor of a figurine, she has used an armature to uphold the practicable stuff, she believes the expedient justified. The novel of Mr. Hodge and Mr. Hazard is an everyday fable; its historical trappings are slight, and it must remain not a disguised biography but a brief symbolic romance of the mind.

Book One: Mr. Hazard

I Funeral of a Mouse

When Mr. Hazard was forty years old, he decided to revisit England. Having been out of it for precisely fifteen years, he had half forgotten its climate; his memory was incurably romantic, and through veils of far-away mist he saw the blackthorn more clearly than the mud. Also, it was true that he, who so dearly loved the sun, had been rather too much in the sun of late. Greece had been fever and chills by turns, and the cave of the chief Odysseus a very rack for broken bones. Missolonghi had been hot in the month of April 1824; a distinguished poet had perished there, and another, less distinguished, had merely had malaria and miraculously neglected to die of it. The month of

May 1825 had been execrably hot, even in the grotto upon the slopes of Mount Parnassus, in the captious opinion of a man mortally wounded. The temperature of such a man has a tropical noon of its own.

If, like Mr. Hazard, you are mortally wounded and yet remain alive, you haven't been mortally wounded after all; you have only the doubtful satisfaction of knowing that there is a pistol ball somewhere behind your collar-bone. In the wet February of 1833 Mr. Hazard began to derive a perverse but gentle pleasure from the conviction that if he continued to grow thinner, he might soon be able to see the pistol ball as plainly as the collar-bone while he shaved by candlelight. He had never yet learned to button his night-shirt properly at the neck.

He had half forgotten the English climate when he landed at London Docks; the channel fogs had been clean as new milk compared to this tarnished verdigris smoke from which the face of his friend Hartleigh emerged with looming eyes like the spread wings of a soft dilapidated bat. The little man was shabby; his coat shared a certain worn furry look with his hair and thick eyelashes.

"My dear friend!" said Mr. Hazard; ten years ago, in Italy, he had cried "My dearest friend!" but now he lacked the requisite breath for the superlative syllable. The fog was heavy as sea-water in his lungs, and a hundred times dirtier in its taste and smell.

"My dear fellow; my dear Hazard!" said Mr. Hartleigh; the beads of fog upon his thick shabby eyelashes grew more salty as he spoke. "And quite, quite unchanged since last we met; what happiness to see you still unchanged!"

"Hah!" said Mr. Hazard incredulously; it was his new way of laughing, which Mr. Hartleigh had never heard before. He supposed, accurately enough, that Hazard had picked it up in Greece; he concluded that modern Greek must be a harsh inhuman tongue.

"That was in '23, before we sailed for the Ionian Islands, I believe," said Mr. Hazard; "I should have thought, you know, that you'd notice a slight difference . . . however, you are yourself looking remarkably well." Which was so palpably untrue that he hastened to add: "And how is the excellent Annamaria?"

"Her health is good at the present moment; considering, you understand," said Mr. Hartleigh to Mr. Hazard, who perfectly understood. He had known Annamaria for a great many years.

"Those delightful winters in Spain and Arabia, with your wife and dear little Lionel," said Mr. Hartleigh, who was oppressed by the silence and by Mr. Hazard's large black hat, "how you must have enjoyed them! Of what inestimable benefit must they have been to your health! And Egypt, too; what did you think of the pyramids? I had hoped you would let me have a sonnet to the pyramids for the *Gossip.*"

"Do you mind if I let down the window a bit?" asked Mr. Hazard. They were now in the hackney-coach; it was undoubtedly an extravagance, but since it was wordlessly agreed between them that the extravagance was Mr. Hazard's, nobody cared in the least about the money. Mr. Hazard was beginning to care rather painfully about the smell; the fancy visited him that the corpse of a mouse might be travelling to London with them in this extravagant hackney-coach.

Mr. Hartleigh glanced fearfully at Mr. Hazard, surprised again by the new and inhuman accent in his voice. "An unmelodious tongue, the modern Greek," thought Mr. Hartleigh in iambic pentameter. Having glanced once more at Mr. Hazard, he decided, not unreasonably, that his friend was about to faint. At the moment they were passing within the curdled nimbus of a street-lamp; Mr. Hartleigh perceived with warm-hearted concern that Mr. Hazard was precisely the colour of a vellum lectionary of the fifteenth century. A few ghostly freckles still lingered upon the thin bridge of his nose, but even these had changed from russet into dun. It was a truly shocking revelation; Mr. Hartleigh let down the window with a bang.

Mr. Hazard said: "Thank you; I prefer the fog to the mouse, don't you?" Mr. Hartleigh realized that Mr. Hazard had not the least intention of fainting; his words were clear and dry as scraps of mica.

Mr. Hartleigh, who had taken a small silver-plated flask from his pocket, put it back again with a thrifty sigh of relief.

"I thought you were ill, but happily it was but the unnatural hue of the fog," he said, his kindly eyes looming bat-like through the dusk.

"It is but the natural hue of my face, unhappily," said Mr. Hazard without apparent regret. "This is the celebrated Missolonghi tint, half-way between tallow and the ship's biscuit. A really hot Arabian sun may toast the biscuit to a more agreeable brown, but this confounded voyage has turned it into toast-and-water. I assure you that I am quite well; I am only concerned lest Annamaria be annoyed with me for sacrificing my appearance to my principles."

"She is certain to admire you; you have the air of a distinguished foreigner," said Mr. Hartleigh, laughing. He was glad that his friend Hazard was not after all about to faint in a hackney-coach, and sincerely glad he had not wasted his brandy upon a fellow who did not care whether he drank cognac or cowslip wine.

Mr Hazard said: "Hah!" which to Mr. Hartleigh's imagination had become modern Greek for a proper English chuckle; he pulled his large black hat over his large and rather alarming eyes and promptly fell asleep. Within the hackney-coach Mr. Hartleigh alone preserved his sharp and waking faculties; the corpse of the mouse and the slumbering form of Mr. Hazard travelled up to London in a darkling stillness equal and profound.

10. 'Tis True 'Tis Pity

When Mr. Hazard descended the narrow stairs of the Hartleighs' house in Marylebone upon the last night of April 1833 he stepped from a confined and breathless atmosphere into a fresh green twilight made chill and wholesome by increasing wind. The currents of air were electric with purpose, and the leaves snapped in the wind like little flags and crackled with cold fire overhead. It was an evening for love or the more severe resolves of ambition; as the breeze lifted the hair from Mr. Hazard's tense contracted forehead, it seemed to lift his heart also, though a moment before his heart had been heavier than a stone.

Now, if ever, was the moment for Mr. Hazard to declare himself a free spirit and a saviour of his kind. Such he had indeed set forth to be, and this with greater energy and impatience than remained in him tonight as he laid his hand upon Hartleigh's front door knob. A hundred fitful and intemperate schemes had flourished and died down within the past twenty years, whose fruits were to benefit the race of man from Niagara to the Straits of Propontis, so many exotics sprung from the fertile soil of Mr. Hazard's brain. His brain had yielded far too many of these harvests; nothing remained of them but chaff and worthless straw. Yet they had cost Mr. Hazard quite as dear as if they had been neatly stored in political granaries, safe from the teeth of rodents, locked away as accomplished laws. The four winds had taken his efforts and scattered them nobody knew where.

Tonight one wind was sufficient to blow an illusion of hope across his brain; it is sad to admit that this hope was concerned with nothing more important than his private happiness. Tonight his opportunity lay before him, had he possessed the strength to seize it, brighter and wider than the dingy street which filled his actual field of vision. Now he had the chance of stepping down four steps into the street, and with the descent entering the England of the time, and setting his thin shoulder to some useful revolution of a wheel in the machine. He did not choose to seize this chance; his fatigue and his indifference persuaded him that all such labours were in vain. He knew that his reputation, his character, his very name were catchwords of conflict and failure; his physical exhaustion prevented him from knowing more, or desiring to know it.

Perhaps if someone had blown a charge upon a key-bugle or chromatic trumpet within Mr Hazard's hearing at that moment, or had forced him to swallow one-twentieth part of a grain of strychnine or six-pennyworth of common brandy, his energies might have been so far recruited as to drive him into unselfish action. Things being as they were, and the street empty, and he tired and stifled by the Hartleighs' conversation, he had no mind except for his private affairs. Strangely and deplorably, these affairs seemed to him of the highest concern. He went down three steps into the street and paused; the influenza had left his body good for nothing more difficult than a night's sleep, but he might have set his mind to some firm and noble purpose. It is sad to record that he did nothing of the sort; he determined to do exactly as he pleased. He looked from side to side, pleased to be alone and to mature his selfish plans in solitude.

He paused, somewhat giddy from his quick descent of the stairs; he closed his eyes for one moment, but in that wink of darkness he had closed his eyes upon the whole world, upon the four remaining months of spring and summer, upon the turmoil of the public heart and the spirit of the time. He was going into the country to mind his own affairs; he was easily spared from the world and its destinies. The world would go round the sun as smoothly and as swiftly without the help of his affection; it could not be hastened or retarded by his pains. Therefore he was wise to leave it, and to live or die as he pleased.

Fortunately for the world, Mr. Hazard's contemporaries were more diligent than he; not one of them was to waste the long, sweet summer as he had determined to waste it. Southey and Lord Ashley were carrying on a correspondence about factory legislation; the first Reform Parliament had lately assembled, Buxton was taking up the work of Wilberforce, Althorpe was amending the poor-laws, and Roebuck bringing forward a vast new scheme of education. Lord John Russell was asking Thomas Moore to go to Ireland with him; "Your being a rebel may somewhat atone for my being a cabinet minister," said Lord John Russell, but Thomas Moore could not go to Ireland after all, because he, poor fellow, had promised to write lives of the literati for Dr. Lardner's *Cabinet Cyclopædia.* Wordsworth was worried about the realm, but delighted with his first grandchild; he was planning a walking tour in Scotland with Crabb Robinson as a holiday, but he would not stop composing Evening Voluntaries while he walked.

Mr. Macauley was writing to his sister from the smoking-room of the House of Commons; in June he would be happy to inform her that in less than a fortnight he would dine with Lord Grey, Mr. Boddington, Mr. Price, Sir Robert Inglis, Lord Ripon, and Lord Morpeth. Everyone was busy and devoted. Young Mr. Whiteley was finishing his pamphlet "Three Months in Jamaica," and the Anti-Slavery Society was awaiting it with eagerness. Wilberforce was dying, and Haydon was painting the Reform Banquet and hearing plenty of excellent stories while he painted. Sometimes these tales were tragic; Sir Charles Bagot told him that Michelangelo's copy of Dante, with a wide margin and his own designs, fell into the hands of the Bishop of Derry and was lost on the passage to Marseilles. There were quantities of new books to offset such losses; Mr. Tennyson's exquisite lyrics, Mr. Browning's *Pauline,* Hartley Coleridge's poems.

Everyone was active for the future. Mr. Landor was preparing to plant thirteen hundred vines at Fiesole, and forty fruit-trees. Lord Nugent was upon the point of sailing for the Ionian Isles. The Oxford Movement was to be set in startling motion by Keble's sermon at Saint Mary's. Mr. Hallam was to die in Vienna, and Mr. Tennyson was to begin writing *In Memoriam.*

Everyone was very energetic. The Greek Islands were in revolt. Hussein Pasha had just left Constantinople for the front, and in the third week in May the ban of outlawry would be launched against Mehemet Ali. A few days later Ibrahim was to break down the gates of Gaza and storm the city of Acre. Upon the eighth of July, the eleventh anniversary of Mr. Shelley's death by drowning, a treaty was to be signed in the palace of Unkiar Skelessi. Meanwhile Mr. Gordon's *History of the Greek Revolution* would be published in London without a single reference to the unfortunate Mr. Hazard.

In France people were having their own adventures. Grisi had pleased the carping Parisian taste as Semiramide. George Sand had met Alfred de Musset at a dinner given by the *Revue des deux mondes;* already they were planning picnics at Fontainebleau; by September they would be *en route* for Venice. Amelie Opie gave tea-parties in the Hôtel de la Paix, wearing a lawn cap with whimpers and crimped frills.

In England everyone was sedulous and earnest. Haydon, going to visit the graves of his children in Paddington New Churchyard, perceived that the name on Mrs. Siddons's headstone was almost obliterated; Malibran was playing at Drury Lane to the enchantment of thousands. After repeated applications the act was finally obtained permitting the extension of the Liverpool and Manchester Railway as far south as Birmingham. Mr. Cobbett had stopped riding about the country, but not before Mr. Trevor had been pelted out of Sunderland with rotten potatoes. Not everyone was lucky, but nearly everyone was industrious. Poor Mrs. Hemans had left her pretty "Dove's Nest" above Windermere and gone to live with her brother in Dublin; she had just sent Dora Wordsworth *The Remains of Lucretia Davidson.* The Wordsworths missed her sadly, but were glad that even in idle Ireland she found time to work.

A few people were very unlucky, but nobody was lazy except Mr. Hazard. He had suffered a severe attack of influenza, but this was not sufficient reason for the complete prostration of his powers of will. If he felt incapable of returning to Greece, he might at least have gone to Limerick, to dissuade Gerald Griffin from joining the Society of Christian Brothers; he might have interested himself in the pathetic fate of John Clare. Mrs. Emmerson had given John Clare a cow, to be called by the charming name of Blossom or May; his cottage at Northborough was thatched, and covered with climbing roses. Nevertheless he was beginning to be haunted by evil spirits; Mr. Hazard, who was familiar with all spirits, might have helped him to exorcise these.

Even the women were working hard this summer; little Miss Landon was particularly hard-working, in her attic room at 22 Hans Place. Although the poor child lived circumspectly, as a boarder in the school establishment of the Misses Lance, she was pursued by cruel slanders; perhaps she was too young and too pretty to escape them save by an incautious dose of prussic acid. Mrs. Norton was busy with the *New Monthly,* and *Friendship's Offering,* and *The Keepsake,* and Mr. Norton was being detestable. Mrs. Shelley had made a sacrifice for Percy in leaving London and going to live at Harrow; she had begun *Lodore,* and undertaken a series of lives of the Italian literati for Dr. Lardner. Hogg's *Shelley Papers* had appeared in the *New Monthly Magazine;* Medwin had written a small volume of *Shelley Papers.* Mary was beginning to believe that she might attempt another edition of the poems, but she knew that Sir Timothy would never consent to a memoir. Leigh Hunt had published *The Mask of Anarchy,* with a preface.

Everyone was changing houses and opinions; Leigh Hunt had gone to Chelsea, and Trelawney had gone to America. When Lady Morgan went to France, her little black harp case was mistaken for a *petit mort* upon its last journey to Père Lachaise.

Coleridge was comfortable in the Gillmans' house at Highgate, but not everyone was so comfortable as Coleridge. Charles Lamb and his sister were living at Bay Cottage, Enfield, a mournful yellow house kept by a woman called Redford. It was believed that this atrocious person locked Miss Lamb in a dark cupboard as a punishment for cutting up a feather-bed and scattering the feathers out of window. Mr. Hazard was to be congratulated upon the superior patience of Mrs. Downing, for his conduct must often have been difficult for even the kindest landlady to understand. He never cut his mattress into pieces, but he frequently spent the night upon the hearth-rug when he did not spend it upon Hampstead Heath. If he had not paid his bills with such regularity, Mrs. Downing would have been glad to know that Mr. Hazard was going into the country to mind his own business and forget the progress of civilization.

CHAPTER THIRTEEN

Short Stories

Gideon's Revenge

Century Magazine, January 1925
Collected Prose of Elinor Wylie. New York: Alfred A. Knopf, 1933

Gideon extinguished the flame wherewith he had lit his pipe; he dropped the match tidily behind the wallflowers, and looked about him with quiet, but incredulous, joy. Standing at the door of the cottage, his head was stooped a little beneath the lintel, partly from actual necessity and partly in a courteous gesture of apology to this exquisite scene in which only children or delicately formed and tinted women might appear appropriate and untarnished. Above him the freshness of the honey-colored thatch contrasted pleasantly with the rose-purple of ancient brick; the watery sheen of the upper windows reflected a few hanging strands of straw, like gilded seaweed observed in the profundity of a wave. Inclosed by its clipped hedge, the garden lay like a small square pool of flowers drawn together in concentrated brightness, as if many larger and grosser gardens had been melted into one and poured into this narrow space. Across the green a dew pond reversed the sky to another pool, and permitted Gideon's vision to plumb without fatigue the utmost depth of the empyrean.

Gideon was a tall old man; his age was perhaps seventy. His face had more of the falcon than the eagle in its lines; the beaked nose, the bony setting of the large, bright eyes, the hollowed cheek and temple, were all carved and polished to a pattern sufficiently bold, but light and restless and uneasy. His eyes were gray; his hair, which had once been reddish, had now the faintly yellowed whiteness of flax; it rose steeply to a crest above his brow. The garments which he wore hung somewhat awkwardly upon his emaciation—an emaciation suggesting austerity rather than weakness. The correct and shabby tweeds were excellent in themselves, molded to fit with easy perfection the scene and circumstance, but although they clothed with tolerable grace the mortal form of Gideon, they did not fit his soul. You saw him preferably in rusty black, with a hat remotely Spanish, and a cloak; decidedly the soul of Gideon wore a black cloak. And indeed at this very moment, within the cottage, Caroline was brushing just such a cloak preparatory to putting it away forever with beautiful cakes of gum camphor crumbling like soft and fragrant ice among its mysterious folds.

Gideon turned and entered the cottage; the rooms appeared deliciously chilled and shadowed by the green orchard to the east. Avoiding the larger chamber, where Caroline whisked fantastic garments into the bland, golden obscurity of a tulip-wood chest of drawers, he turned into the kitchen and surveyed its cool and ordered colors with minute approval. It was a room decorous and subtly bright, a place for the concoction of junkets and cherry-pies. Gideon sighed with pleasure; it was a miracle that he, a lawless, bitter man, should have imagined this room and made it. Of course there had been the skeleton ready to his hand—the stone floor, the beams, the fireplace—but he had breathed upon cold ashes, and they had flowered like a domestic rose.

Caroline had climbed the steep little stairs to the attic; he could hear portmanteaus bumping about overhead, like huge frolicsome beasts; he had a sudden picture of the trim, pink-faced servant surrounded by portmanteaus and kit-bags, labeled in dusty, barbaric scarlet, enormous in the gloom. He reflected with satisfaction that all his papers were already neatly pigeonholed in his grandfather's desk and his mother's boule cabinet; Caroline was merely rummaging among ponchos and sombreros.

Slowly, with a fastidious, yet sensual, savoring of his delights, Gideon entered the other room and strolled down its entire length, stopping here and there to touch the lovely surface of wood perversely satin-skinned, or velvet worn and rosy as immemorial lichen. Here again was something more than human in the happy confluence of various times and manners; he had seen these objects scattered in obscure exile among the Victorian ineptitudes of his mother's vast drawing-rooms, or lately huddled ignominiously in storage warehouses; he had purchased some of them carelessly at the ragged ends of the earth, and now they were gathered together under the green and glazing twilight of the apple-trees to make a miraculous whole. He had bought a cottage, knocked down a partition or two, and engaged a certain number of pantechnicon vans; he had expected the place to be comfortable and rather absurd, and by some curious necromancy of chance it was grave and exquisite. It was as if it had always been so, and his. Between open windows, his desk was flooded by calm radiance.

As he fingered the firmly packed bundles of letters, bound with pink legal tape, or more sentimentally confined by blue ribbons, he considered the future with approval. It was eminently fitting; it was, indeed, inevitable. How, save under conditions of the most shining peace, could he hope to relax into that judicial clarity of mind so necessary to his great project? The hardships, the astringent horrors of his past career, had precisely steeled his hand to execution; it now remained for a poor, but honest, gentleman to judge the culprits before killing them, and Gideon was acutely aware of the propriety of being equitable to begin with, if only to augment the pleasure of being savage in the final sentence, the final act of revenge.

He stared retrospectively down the lurid vista of the last twenty-five years, his mind's eye blinking, for all its falcon look, in the full chemical glare of recollection. There had been, quite literally, singularly little sunlight in the vista, and that little had quivered to a tropical intensity removed by several continents from this subaqueous glimmer stained by apple-trees. But mostly, he remembered, things had happened at night; that was, perhaps, the reason he had achieved so flattering and profitable a reputation as special correspondent.

Special! Oh, very special indeed! For who but Gideon would have been clever enough to be forever on the spot, the often bloody and unhealthy spot, where things were happening at night? What other nocturnal vigilance had so well observed, what vitriolic pen recorded, alike the curious minutiæ and the vast apocalypse of life? From the beginning to the end of that bewildering vista he had contrived to see the event strangely, and to make the strangeness vivid by his words. Also, he had advanced in wisdom and cunning; he recalled with contempt how crudely he had daubed hell-fire and sanguine upon his earlier efforts. In ninety-eight, when he had seen the *Maine* intemperately uncurl a million fronds of brilliance against the plushy dark, he could not, telling the dreadful thing beheld, curdle the reader's veins as now his lightest, coolest whisper curdled them. The latest of all his writings, the wry, amused account of Lenine stretched upon his crimson upholstery under the great glass bell like some horrible wax flower, blooming through unnatural, and electric, days, that was excellent, that was art.

2

And now, the quarter-century past, he was quit of restraint, of delicacies and decencies; now he was free of galling sacred vows and public scruples. The very last of the Pennimans had died twenty years ago in the person of old Joseph; Gideon had kept his promise to Millicent, and Millicent herself had been dead for twenty-five years.

He was free to turn that intricate and fiery engine, his mind, upon the people he had hated and had, for a measured space of time, striven to forget. At first, after his wife's death, he had acidly regretted his promise to her—the promise given to the expiring appeal of her large blue eyes, but never ratified by their wedded spirits in this world or the vaguer one into whose ambiguities she had at once departed. He had kept the promise because it was a promise; he had been totally untrammeled by sympathy for its purpose or its beneficiaries. He had spared the Pennimans for a score of years; he had not written a book, no, not so much as an epitaph upon any of them until two decades had yellowed the latest of their tombs. It had been a hellish bore, but now he was glad he had refrained. The long and lenten abstinence from revenge had but given edge to his appetite and sharpened his powers to austere perfection.

Gideon drew a dozen slim and pointed pencils from a drawer of the desk; upon its dark-amber surface he placed a formidable pile of copy-paper. The book loomed before his happy contemplation, tremendous, Protean, monstrous, yet alluring. A book, but not alone a book; a mighty chase, a dexterous unmasking, a trial, and an execution. And Gideon, at once Justice incarnate and the instrument of Justice, Gideon must be both judge and executioner. The book was to be a headsman's ax, savage, medieval, elegant, and efficient. Then, picturing a row of Penniman faces upon the spikes of Temple Bar, Gideon smiled a slight abstemious smile.

Apart from fancies, however charming, the facts were these; he reviewed them swiftly, leaning back luxuriously in a chair whose polished curves were as velvet to his neuralgic bones. The book was a debt to his own soul, long overdue, heavy with accretion of interest. He had waited, for Millicent's darling and ridiculous sake, until all kith and kin of hers were moldered into complete indifference. She had desired to shield them from anger and annoyance, for surely their fatted, gelded souls were incapable of pain; she had interposed her threadbare little body between their torpor and his vengeance. Very well; it had been so, but now he would remember it all, and set it down, and verily the page should shrivel beneath the fire of his revelation. Though they skulked in their sepulchers, shrouded in this their last cowardice, he would burn them out of oblivion; the flame of their destruction should ascend forever, purified and fervent, sweet in the nostrils of the brave. He would tell the tale; he would release that holy indignation which for so long had made his heart a fever.

Milly—that foolish nickname wherein her family, with characteristic impertinence, had clothed the golden pallor of her girlhood! If Gideon pronounced her name he enriched the vowels with a foreign inflection which made it more Melisande than Millicent. That was her proper appellation, that long soft veil of sound, fitting her sallow-flaxen beauty with an enduring garment.

She, who had lain so long asleep in his heart, should be brought forth once more into the wide, bright chamber of his mind; he would look at her in the unpitying glare of that illumination. She would stand, willowy and disarming, lovely and ineffectual, beside the solid, stolid forms of her murderers, the Pennimans. Gideon would look at them all; the Pennimans would tremble and grow pale, they would even grow thin perhaps; Millicent would smile. It would not be the smile of her later days, painted narrow and colorless by despair; it would be the smile of the beginning, of hope and casual courage and unconsidered joy. Gideon ground his teeth, thinking how the Pennimans had destroyed her gaiety and trust. She had loved her father and mother; she had even loved the unspeakable Ambrose, with his long nose and liquid, languid eyes; by love she had been broken and undone.

Of course they had opposed the match; they were obstructive by instinct and conviction, and Gideon, who had refused to be a barrister in order to write for the lesser journals, was sufficiently above them in family and below them in fortune to irritate their every prejudice. His wit inflamed their mental tissues like cayenne pepper; his tongue was gall and vinegar. They resented his height and were half afraid of his hair, which was never properly brushed; he seemed an enigma designed to insult them; his doing could not be other than wrong, but his mere being was the radical error. Gideon knew that, and the reflection soothed him; it meant that he had always, even without trying, done his best to please them: his best must always fail with the Pennimans, and he was glad he had not tried too hard. Millicent had tried too hard, and, in foredoomed endeavor, been destroyed.

He had been a strange son-in-law for the Pennimans; he had fluttered that dove-cote with a vengeance. Fat pigeons they were, and Ambrose with the melting gaze of a turtle above his little waistcoat's curve. And Millicent among them, white and fluttering, with her perpetual olive branch: she was truly a dove!

Without the Pennimans, pecking and obese, how far might they not have flown together, Gideon and Millicent, the falcon and the dove! God knew she had always wanted to be free; God had known it all along, in fact, and that was Gideon's quarrel with God, second only to his quarrel with the Pennimans. For the Deity, frequently invoked by that pious family, had apparently been moved by their flatteries rather than by Gideon's dignified silence; God had not saved Millicent even at the last minute: he had, by allowing her to die, given her back to the Pennimans. Gideon, who had never believed in God, found this impossible to forgive; in his indignation he realized that he was a Christian.

The Pennimans, outrageous to the last, had always blamed him for his wife's death; they had pecked her into shreds while he was cynically examining the Spanish-American War. They had not even taken the trouble to cable news of her illness; he had returned to find her *in extremis.* Gideon was frantic; the Pennimans were sorrowful and mildly complacent. They expressed surprise at his reappearance, and disgust at what they were pleased to term his neglect. Millicent had, apparently, been killed by the absence of a husband whose presence had always, according to the Pennimans, constituted a criminal menace to her health and sanity. The bronze door of the Penniman vault shut firmly upon her mortal remains; the family, in solemn conclave, decided that Gideon was sailing for South Africa with Milly's blood upon his hands. Gideon knew that their own hands were dabbled in her innocence.

Gideon found the South African War a personal convenience, but against the Pennimans he was very bitter, and his amazing despatches, colored and brilliant with hate, were only a partial relief to his feelings. He found it impossible to dislike the Boers with the authentic fervor so desirable in a special correspondent; quite deliberately he dipped his pen into his private gall before writing, and his passionate loathing for a respectable family at Wimbledon fired half England to a pure flame of patriotism. But it was all very unsatisfactory and rather troublesome, this inner pretense that Cronje and Wessels were in reality Mrs. Penniman and Ambrose. His despatches were devoured raw by the popular appetite, but he himself went hungry; he starved for his revenge. Gideon, remembering those days, laughed heartily. How fierce he had been, and how frustrate!

The sunlight fell across his dusky golden desk, and still he remembered, and did not write. That was twenty-five years ago, and this was England, and he was old, but neither frustrate nor starving. The Gideon of the Transvaal had been a widowed Gideon of forty-odd, bereaved and raging—a Gideon who had but just observed the wife of his romantic youth go down to the grave shrunken to premature decay, quenched in body and soul, the clear flame withered, the bright stem trodden underfoot. For a long and parching term of years he had beheld her obliquely in the flawed mirror of her dying face; later he had shut his eyes while she slept in his heart. Now he looked at her again, in the cool and blessed light of these windows, in the peace of this quiet room; she was a girl again, and beautiful. But Millicent had always been beautiful.

It was the other Pennimans who had been ugly; how ugly he shuddered to recall. He drew a packet of papers toward him. These were photographs of the criminals, letters from Milly, letters from Ambrose, his own wild scrawls. Gideon adjusted his spectacles.

3

At seven o'clock Caroline lit the lamp; it was a pale unluminous yellow against the western window-panes, where rose color was fading. Half an hour later she placed a small tray at Gideon's elbow; the noiseless hand was also skilful, for the cutlet was done to a turn, the coffee superlative. Gideon ate and drank, thanking the stars now set in chrysoprase above the apple-trees. At nine he put down the last of the letters and, lifting one of the photographs, examined it intently. A curious trembling seized him; he appeared a prey to obscure emotions, and his face was visibly convulsed.

The picture, a highly glazed *carte-de-visite* of the eighties, showed a family group augmented by one stranger: it showed, clearly enough, the Pennimans and Gideon. There, seated side by side, were old Joseph and his wife; at their feet was Ambrose; behind them, poised as if for flight, the less substantial forms of Gideon and Millicent wavered against a painted frieze of foliage. The faces were remarkably distinct–distinct as the golden syllables of Harrogate bitten into grayish cardboard below them.

The photograph completed at a single shattering blow the annihilation of Gideon's hard-won calm. The tears poured from his eyes upon the glassy countenance of Ambrose, while Gideon laughed and laughed.

Here, presented upon a little slip of grimy cardboard, was the whole stupendous farce; the farce was here reduced to such miniature proportions that the human eye could grasp it and the human understanding contain it without effort. During the last three hours, while letter after letter passed into the relentless illumination of his mind, Gideon had gradually perceived the outlines of this farce; they were at first too huge for his comprehension. But now, under the complacent glow of the lamp, the picture made them very plain, very clear and definite.

The Pennimans were funny, and he was a fool. They had always been funny, and he had always been a blazing fool not to see it. They were harmless and absurd; any one with eyes in his head could see that now. Joseph was funny and innately charming; a perfect Cruikshank portrait of a blustering, heavy father born fifty years too late. Mrs. Penniman was funny and pathetic and rather a dear; yes, she was entirely a dear, with her cotton-wool hair and her face like a frightened baby's. And Ambrose was funny, and–well, Ambrose was enormously funny; Gideon left it at that. As for Millicent and Gideon, they were funniest of all; they were, he realized, tremendous.

There was Milly——and oh, how right the Pennimans had been to call her Milly!—there she was, in her famous green silk frock from Liberty's, looking like a Du Maurier drawing executed not in ink, but in China tea, the sweet little ghost of a Du Maurier drawing. How sweet she looked, and how extraordinarily silly! Yes, of course, that was the word; that was precisely it—silly Milly, adorably silly Milly, clinging to the arm of her devoted young husband. To the stalwart arm? Perhaps not quite to the stalwart arm, but at least to the protecting arm of a fiercely possessive Gideon in the first of the black cloaks, with the biggest and blackest of all the sombreros pulled down over smoldering eyes, whose expression was accurately compounded of love for his bride and haughty malevolence for the rest of the world. Which meant, mostly the Pennimans. No wonder poor Ambrose lifted his own eyes in alarm to the face of his tall brother-in-law.

Was it possible that he had ever believed himself a suitable husband for that delightful little idiot in green silk and Italian corals who was so obviously made of pink sugar candy? Both sun and rain must inevitably melt the pretty creature; the chills and ardors of common life must reduce her to crumbs of sugary dust. Brittle and soft and sweet, Milly was always sweet. Oh, he had loved her right enough, and she had loved him; but Milly had loved every one, and Gideon had loved no one but Milly.

Was it possible that he had ever expected the Pennimans to understand his plans, his ambitions, for Milly and himself? He laughed again to remember the mixture of frigid courtesy and contempt with which he had invariably met their suggestions and advice. He might as well have worn a black mask in addition to the outrageous sombrero for all he had ever let them see of his thoughts or intensities of feeling. Not that it mattered; he was such piercing vinegar to their emollient oil. It was nobody's fault: they were all of them good and kind; Milly was an angel, a sugar angel; and the young, then, eager Gideon no more than an impulsive and infatuated fool. What a fool he had been to burden himself with such confectionary! What a fool she had been to intrust herself to his hot and sticky grasp! It was a miracle that they had survived so long in each other's strange company.

Gideon again bent his falcon gaze upon the photograph, and his laughter was quenched in pity. The people in the picture were all so ridiculous and serious and profoundly innocent, and now he might laugh at them as much as he liked. He could never laugh with them, and it was nobody's fault.

And the book? Gone, like a gorgeous thunder-cloud, tiger-streaked, into profound oblivion. Dead, like the Pennimans, who, in its death, were prodigally revenged.

Gideon stooped, and set a match to the fire. It flew upward like a sanguine flower, and the room was roseate instead of amber-yellow in the lamp-light. Its colors glowed from new planes and facets; its shapes were subtly altered and enhanced. Caroline came in quietly with the whisky and soda.

Presently Gideon rose, and lit his pipe. A tall and solitary figure, he stood gazing into the lambent mystery of the fire; he sighed gently.

"I suppose I shall have to learn to dislike my neighbors," he told himself in a low voice. "One might write a grim realistic novel about those squat dark people at Skatt's Farm."

Abut at the back of his mind was a sick conviction that they were probably quite pleasant, harmless people, and after a little while he took his candlestick from the hall table and went upstairs to bed.

He jumped very quickly between the cool sheets, and fell asleep trying hard to hate the squat dark people at Skatt's Farm. But the dreadful part of it was that Gideon could not hate them.

The Life Story of Lydia Greensmith

New Republic, November 24, 1926
Collected Prose of Elinor Wylie. New York: Alfred A. Knopf, 1933

They could not have had a more delicious day for the Grand Prix if they had ordered it beforehand, leaving time for at least three fittings, from Patou or Poiret. Therefore I had made fairly certain of not meeting an American at the Musée Carnavalet; the sudden vision of Miss Lydia Greensmith was a miraculous shock to my nerves. These were already slightly shaken, because the cabman had cursed so very heartily when he discovered that I was not, after all and in spite of my new ashen-rose-colored raiment, for Longchamps and the races. I stood staring at the glass case with its little dusty dead rats and their goblin printing-press and thinking that art is long, perhaps, but excessively thin. I was alone save for the sinister plaster presences in the next room and the scarcely more vivacious creature selling postcards to nobody at the door. Then Lydia Greensmith entered from the garden and I was amazed into a voice.

"Oh," I said, "*Oh!*" She was so charming and so absurd, from the enameled pansy at her throat to her small elastic-sided boots, and she was obviously too soft to be plaster and too warm to be wax.

"Bonjour, mademoiselle," she said politely and I trust quite sincerely. It is true that my great-grandmother was a Huguenot, and one does not expect to meet an American at the Carnavalet on the day of the Grand Prix. The moment she spoke I perceived that she came from Connecticut.

"Do let me help you with that heavy bag," I cried at once, seizing it by its worn handle. "And your box, goodness gracious, you haven't been dragging a great leather box across the courtyard, have you? Isn't there a porter somewhere about?"

"At the races," said Miss Greensmith sadly. "You see, I tipped them all last night; the chambermaid, too. It's always a mistake; one gets no service the next day. A taxi, perhaps."

"The animal at the door might find one," I suggested, but she shook her head.

"Really they're all cross with me for leaving," she murmured. "I know it's flattering, but so awkward about the bags. And you, my dear . . . no, really, you mustn't spoil your pretty gloves. But if you could see whether there is a taxi in the street . . ."

"There is," I said, "mine; it's waiting for me. May I take you anywhere?"

"I thought I would go first to the brasserie on the corner, for a 'fine,'" Miss Greensmith replied timidly. "It's melancholy, this parting. . . . Goujon's darling lions . . . Ah me, how I shall miss it all! I've been very happy; I've loved it so, you see; perhaps I'm making a mistake." And she began to cry.

"A 'fine' is indicated," I thought. Aloud I said, "I'll tell the taxi man to keep an eye on your luggage."

"Please," she whispered. "But are you quite sure, my dear, that the man's reliable? I have one or two little trifles . . ."

"Not from the Carnavelet?" I asked; I couldn't help it. The bag had seemed mysteriously heavy. We turned into the rue des Francs-Bourgeois.

"Only from the cellars, child, and gifts, all of them; gifts from the government. Defective pieces; broken fans and bits of porcelain. It's a matter of sentiment, entirely, but so kind of the Ministers to understand."

"But do you mean," I cried, when we were seated at the small green table with a "fine" between us, "that you were actually living there?"

"Yes," said Miss Greensmith simply.

"No," I said to the waiter. "I prefer an infusion. Camomile. Better for the nerves."

"They permitted it out of pure kindness, and because my uncle had been Governor of Connecticut. Yes, the fact that I am a gentlewoman undoubtedly had something to do with it, but that doesn't alter the circumstances of their amazing kindness."

"You're very pretty, you know," I said somewhat impertinently. It was true; she had enormous lavender-gray eyes in a fragile three-cornered face. I guessed that her curls had once been dark, but now they were silvery and shining with a moonlight fairness.

"That has nothing to do with it," she answered with an air of pride and soft reproof. "It was pure altruistic kindness on the part of the Ministers, I assure you. I asked the government if I might, mentioning my uncle and a few distinguished ancestors, and I was allowed to live in three small rooms in the attic. No modern conveniences, of course, but an exquisite view. It is not generally known; I hope you will not speak of it, my dear, particularly as I am leaving."

"Ah, such a lovely, lovely place to live! How have you the heart to leave it?" I demanded. "Remember the quiet courtyard and the sunlight on the frosty stone, and the rooms as clear and elegant as the inner shapes of flowers! Remember the little coach and horses carved from mother of pearl and gold, and you might look at it every single hour! Ah, but you were lucky, and I think you are rather an idiot to go home!"

"I liked the earrings made in the form of a guillotine even better," said Miss

Greensmith wistfully. "Only, my dear, I'm not going home to America, you see. I've had quite enough of the Grand Central Station, thank you.

"Yes, I was born in Connecticut; you are entirely right about that," she continued shyly. "Near Fairfield; pleasant country, especially in the spring. Lilacs and apple-blossoms; there was a hedge of white lilacs before the door. But I was always afraid to go out of the door; I never was properly adventurous until I grew up. I rarely left the house until I was past thirty, and then only in the cool of the evening, in a blonde lace veil. Ours was a huge old house; the roofs were as broad and green as other people's front lawns, and one hot summer I had actually a little garden of lilies of the valley in the shade of the north chimney. The peaks and gables used to rise above me like green hills; they were covered with moss, and the treetops made other hills beyond them."

"But why did you go away?" I asked. "And what about the Grand Central Station? Another 'fine'?"

"Please," said Miss Greensmith. "A l'eau. Well, my child, my dear parents died for one thing, and my brother married a film star. I did not care for the curtains she selected for the drawing-room, and I thought I might be happier in New York."

"And were you?" I inquired, pouring out another cup of camomile tea.

"I never saw New York," said Miss Greensmith, "except from the Grand Central Station. I never dared to venture into the street. I lived in the Grand Central Station for fifteen years.

"I arrived before it was really finished," she went on, "and at first it was somewhat uncomfortable, but I soon grew accustomed to it, and then for a time I was very happy. It was beautiful, you know, in a queer way; that great floor glittering like golden ice, and all the strange long corridors and lighted galleries. And then the shops; I did enjoy the shops, I must confess."

"But where did you sleep?" I asked rather nervously, sipping my infusion.

"Oh, at the Biltmore, sometimes, and sometimes at the Commodore, and then towards the end I tried the Roosevelt for a change," said Miss Greensmith with a pensive smile.

"Didn't you ever have the curiosity to go to the Belmont?"

"I considered it, but I couldn't bring myself to cross Forty-second Street, my dear," Miss Greensmith admitted, sighing. "But what did it matter, with my whole world under one vast zodiacal roof? I had everything I needed for that fifteen years."

"Then you must know that little shop where I used to have tea with William, and the buttermilk place, and the place where they sell Irish dulse, and the secret entrance from the Yale Club!"

"But naturally," said Miss Greensmith, "I know it all; nobody else knows it as I do. But of course I prefer the Carnavalet."

"I can quite comprehend that," I answered sympathetically. "And now you are leaving it forever. Why? In the name of all adorable gimcracks, why?"

"I am going to Rome, " said Miss Greensmith. "Not over, you know; I am an Episcopalian. Just to Rome."

"'Which is the sepulchre . . . '" I said. "'Go thou to Rome, at once the Paradise . . . '"

"Precisely," Miss Greensmith replied. "That is precisely what I mean."

"Oh, is it, really and truly?" I cried, trembling a little in spite of the camomile tea. "But do you mean what I mean, I wonder? Is that the reason you are going to Rome?"

"Yes, said Miss Greensmith, "the Protestant cemetery." And she began to cry.

"Don't," I begged her, which was unfair, because I also had begun to cry.

"The authorities have given me permission," she whispered finally, touching her wet lashes with a cobweb handkerchief. "I shall sit there all day long, every day for the rest of my life. 'From the world's bitter wind, seek shelter in the shadow . . . ' I love the adorable gimcracks of the Carnavalet, but I believe I've outgrown them, just as I outgrew Connecticut and the Grand Central Station. I don't care for anything now, except–except the Protestant cemetery. And in the evening I shall drink Asti Spumante and read . . . "

"Of course," I said, "you're quite right. I think, if you don't mind, I shall go to Rome with you. But first, you must come with me to the Ritz Bar to have a champagne cocktail."

"Yes," said Miss Lydia Greensmith, "I'd like to do that, my dear. Only don't forget that we've left my luggage at the Carnavalet."

Then, as I went to fetch it, she took a volume of Shelley out of her reticule and laid it upon the little green table. The book fell open in the middle, where the blue silk marker divided the enchanted leaves.

"Another 'fine,' if you please," I heard her murmur to the waiter in her French of Fairfield in Connecticut.

CHAPTER FOURTEEN

Articles and Reviews

"Excess of Charity"

New York Herald Tribune, Books, February 27, 1927
Collected Prose of Elinor Wylie. New York: Alfred A. Knopf, 1933

Ever since I have known Roger Ingpen, I have wished that Shelley might have had him for friend; it would have been so great a happiness to each to know the other. But, as things have fallen out in this middling world, Shelley's loss is the greater, since in all ways of the heart and mind Roger Ingpen does, of course, know Shelley very well, whereas Shelley himself had to be content with such persons as the shadowy Dr. Lind, of Windsor, and that most execrable of mentors, William Godwin. Nevertheless, even Shelley is fortunate in this friendship, sundered as it is by a hundred years from the look into the living eyes and the clasp of the actual hand; he is lucky to have Mr. Ingpen for his editor, the executor as it were of his spiritual effects and the rich estate of his immortal soul.

It is not necessary to believe in a future life in order to call Shelley's soul immortal. He lives continuously and increasingly in the intellects and the affections of those who love him. While I would desire a true eternity for Shelley, a stretch of time made smooth enough and golden enough to foster his capacity for joy, it is evident that even without heaven his essence survives in the quickened blood of a child who reads for the first time the "Ode to the West Wind" and runs across an autumn field shouting its words to the air; it is evident that it survives in steady brightness in the brain of a scholar such as Mr. Ingpen. Francis Thompson has certain unforgivable words to say of the cold and bitter quality of an immortality such as this; he is indeed fortunate if he has found a better paradise for himself. It is possible to-day, after the long lapse of a century dimmed by the smoke of soft coal and the fumes of petroleum, to find more friends of Shelley's among your casual acquaintances than remained by his breathing side during the course of his brief existence.

It is possible to walk along Sixth Avenue under the spiteful thunder of the "L" and, meeting a man whom you have known only slightly, to have that man within half an hour put into your hands a letter from Shelley to Peacock. It is possible to discover in talking with this man that he feels precisely as you do about the character of Shelley and is as indifferent as you to the danger of being considered a lunatic. "I live over again the days of my infancy and youth . . ."; so runs the beginning of this letter, written in Bath upon some September day, and as this man and I read it together, the days of Shelley's infancy and youth are relived for a third time in our minds. It is possible to be sitting one morning above the petty clatter of a typewriter and to have a messenger give you a note from a friend which miraculously incloses a check upon Messrs. Brookes and Company, of Chancery Lane, and this check is drawn in favor of W. Godwin, Esq., and signed Percy Bysshe Shelley; this particular excess of charity is for the sum of forty pounds, and the cold old bloodsucker received it from the boy upon a January day in the year 1818. So again it becomes a symbol of generosity, this time for my more grateful benefit. It is possible to sit among beloved companions a few winter evenings later, and setting this frail slip of paper too suddenly before the eyes of a high lyrical poet, to see those green eyes fill with tears as at the evocation of a spirit. These things are possible by the chances of every day; if they were miracles they would not be half so kind. It is possible to meet a woman with a singularly musical name who has driven her little car across the downs to dine at a great house in Wiltshire and to have her say to you before two hours have passed, "If you and I had been alive we might have done something." You may look at her by the pale rose-colored light of a late June sunset and shake your head and reply, "I doubt it; I very much doubt it," thinking how powerless you would have been in the adamantine face of the Lord Chancellor and the "Quarterly Review"; yet even this lovely nonsense seems a sort of immortality.

It is even possible, by a sort of divine good luck, to sit for long delighted hours in a house in Bedford Park, listening to the editor of the Julian Edition of Shelley, and occasionally interrupting him to cap a quotation from a letter, and smiling with him at a hundred beloved recollections of some one we have never seen. I have wondered what other fraternity of interest may constitute so strong a bond or so infallible a test of liking, and I have thought that fishermen must come next, with your true veteran golfers a poor third. For this is "shop" of the most intoxicating kind; "a bright fire, a clean hearth, and the rigor of the game," might be its motto, although those charming words were written about whist players. It is pleasant to drink champagne cocktails in Paris while you talk about the shoes of the Princess de Lamballe, but it is far, far pleasanter to drink tea in Bedford Park while you talk about the youthful "printing freaks" or Mr. Shelley or the beautiful silk pantaloons he wore when he came home for the holidays. The laughter of the unskilful and the grieved sighs of the judicious cannot persuade me that I have ever been happier than upon certain evenings in that house, with a cup of tea in my hand at the proper early-nineteenth-century hour, and in my lap and laid on either side of me a shining treasure of scrap-books and manuscripts and pictures. And this volatile inebriation has illuminated the chill white tunnels leading underground to Charing Cross; it has sung among the wheels of the last tired train to London.

It is possible to lie upon heaven-scented pine-needles under the smooth blue crystal of Monadnock and to read that surprising book, "Shelley and the Unromantics" with sentiments of admiration and wonder not unmixed with shame. This book was written by a woman, Olwen Ward Campbell, and it is a curious fusion of elements, a subtle and sensitive vision of Shelley set strangely beside a rather cruel and intolerant view of all his friends. I can hate Godwin as a Catholic hates Judas, and I cannot love Godwin's daughter, Mary, but Mrs. Campbell will not even forgive Hogg his passing treachery or Peacock his constitutional coldness. I wish I might be so fastidious, but Hogg and Peacock will always win me to themselves, however imperfect they may have proved as friends of Mr. Shelley's. Nevertheless, this book is revealing and beautiful, and its discovery was pleasant and profitable to my mind. I do most passionately agree with its conclusions as to Shelley; of those who never knew him in life, only Browning and Swinburne have spoken with an equal understanding, and since their words are after all more magnificent than Mrs. Campbell's, perhaps their comprehension is a little less. Her book is further precious in that its author is patently a very good person; too few of those who love him have done him sufficient honor in this respect. The beauty of this bad thought must be that Shelley would not have been likely to be hard upon our faults. I cannot pardon Francis Thompson for his damnable patronage, or Canon Kingsley for his brute stupidity, or Matthew Arnold for his blindness; Mrs. Campbell cannot pardon those "people of obvious instability of temperament and unsuitability to life" who have loved Shelley as such men failed to love him. But the happy chances are that Shelley would have forgiven the lot of us and the tangle of our loves and dislikes; this is his "excess of charity."

To me the most valuable tributes to Shelley must come from fine and virtuous persons like Mr. Ingpen and Mrs. Campbell; this is the praise best worth his taking, though not the only praise which might have pleased him. It weighs more heavily in the scales against detraction than a dozen romantic essays or half a hundred sonnets. So among the various magics of Mr. Yeats's "Autobiographies" it was a joyful shock to come upon such high eulogy of "Prometheus," as it was a dull distress to learn the long-suspected secret that Dowden's smaller spirit could not lift itself into a true approval of the marvelous creature whose life he has recorded with mild uncritical tact.

If you really love Shelley you are not uncritical; you do not need to be. "For"—to paraphrase Swinburne's words about his Queen of Scots—"surely he was something better than innocent." Is it then necessary to pretend that he was never mistaken, never reckless, never forgetful of others as he was so often forgetful of himself? When Shelley was nineteen he was actually in many ways a ridiculous though lovable and a brilliant child; he had already a mind like his own solar microscope, yet his wild imagination and impulsive nature, together with what he would himself have called "the delicacy of his constitution," led him into absurdities and cruelties such as the Hitchener affair. By the time he was twenty-nine he had grown so wise, so patient and so kind that to any superstitious person his drowning must appear inevitable. If any ten years of the world have ever witnessed a more amazing development and flowering of nobility from imperfection, I should be glad to celebrate that decade in letters of pure silver.

The theory that Shelley was completely unaware of his own defects seems to me especially preposterous. By the circumstances of his life he was caught up into a situation where any loud bewailing of the past, any open self-reproaches or laments would have cut a living woman to the heart and left a dead one none the better for her revenge. Both Hunt and Peacock knew something of the lively and voracious wolf which the boy carried under his cloak until he died; to admit to Mary a remorse for Harriet's suicide would have been a form of self-indulgence more distasteful to Shelley than all the bottles of claret which Byron swallowed in his shaken presence in that fantastic house in Pisa.

It is an ironical comment on the impossibility of pleasing every one, or indeed any one, that while Shelley is often criticized for his hardness of heart and lack of warm humanity, and this apparently upon the strength of the undoubted truth that he continued to live and to write divine poetry and brilliant letters even after he had made some grave and tragic errors of judgment, he is also often criticized for being over-sensitive and over-sad, and this upon the strength, which is called weakness, of his mood in such poems as "Stanzas Written in Dejection" and "Lines Written Among the Euganean Hills." As a matter of fact he was extraordinarily courageous about his sufferings both physical and mental, but the poems rather than the letters represent the personal essence of his soul. He could always be depended upon to write Peacock a masterly description of the Coliseum or Mary a tender admonition to be a good girl and get along with her novel, but he could not depend upon his own spirit never to fail him in secret, he could not always be so charitable to himself as he invariably was to his friends. It is hard to realize, now that the least of his lyrics seems written in starry gold upon the mind, that in those moments when his hand of flesh and blood scribbled them upon paper, his own mind never dreamt of such consummation; he believed that very few people would ever read these words and fewer still would cherish them.

Now if in turn you cannot believe this moving wonder, you have only to look at his own letters to have it proved to your entire satisfaction or despairing pity, according to your temperament and habit of thought. He truly believed that few would read his verses, and he hid them from Mary for fear of wounding her, as she herself will tell you in her "Note for the Poems Written in 1818." It is comforting to read the end of this; "but with one or two that he loved, he gave way to wild and joyous spirits, or in more serious conversation expounded his opinions with vivacity and eloquence."

Somewhere, and I am almost glad that I have not the time to turn to the actual letter, Shelley writes of himself that there are a dozen persons at most who regard him with anything but hatred and contempt. This is a strange and melancholy thing to set beside Hunt's description of Shelley; the words are not Hunt's but Lord Bacon's, and for aught I know Hunt may misquote them. "Excess of charity, and it is not possible that man or angel should come in danger by it."

Perhaps not ultimate danger. Certainly there is no danger to-day that Shelley may not be beloved. But this "excess of charity" made his life more vulnerable than most, and it is pleasant to consider his reward in the opinion of the future. His future is already our own past. Some of us have loved him for longer years than composed the span of his whole life. Roger Ingpen told me that he bought his first book of Shelley's poems when he was fourteen years old, or was it twelve? At least he said to me generously: "You see you beat me." I did. I first read "The Cloud" and "The Skylark" in my Third Reader, and I think I was seven years old. This was the same winter when my innocent young mother read "Christabel" aloud to me. My admiration for it was so nearly pure horror that "The Skylark" was a great consolation after dark. "If we were things born not to shed a tear"; even a child can understand those words. Then when I was eleven we were no longer in that Victorian high-ceiled house in Philadelphia, where "The Skylark" first sang to me. It was September in Washington and the air was warm and sweet as if all the grapes and peaches of Maryland and Virginia had flavored it to my taste. I stood before the smallest bookcase in the library, and from its shelves I drew Trelawney's "Recollections." The window was wide open; there was plenty of light and soft autumnal wind in the room. I did not move except to turn the pages. Even the black leather chair was too far away from the scene within the covers of the book. I stood quite still and turned the pages, and the curtains blew in at the window and a few golden leaves blew in between them.

So I read for the first time of Shelley's death and burial. I can remember what I felt in that moment of past time, but never what I thought. It is therefore impossible to tell of it except to draw the picture of the room full of light and softer air and of the child standing in the center of the room and turning the pages of the book, afraid to move, afraid to cry for fear the scene within the pages of the book might be hidden from her eyes, wondering and wondering why the bright creature who had lived within that scene should have died and fallen into dust no stronger than the golden leaves blowing in at the window.

Path of the Chameleon. A review of W. B. Yeats's *Autobiographies: Reveries Over Childhood and Youth* and *The Trembling of the Veil.*

New York Herald Tribune, Books, February 13, 1927
Collected Prose of Elinor Wylie. New York: Alfred A. Knopf, 1933

These chapters of a single symmetrical book compose one of the great poetic romances of the world. I had meant to say, one of the great romantic novels, but as my dazzled eyes withdrew themselves from the final page I knew that the word was too frivolous and too unspiritual. Nevertheless, for all its dignity and verisimilitude, the book has the luminous visionary inner strangeness of the higher legends and fabulous tales of antiquity, and this together with the fine simplicity of truth. These far-off things are not older than the short half of a century nor these battles longer ago than the other day, but they have become one with some imperishable fabric of mythology by virtue of their own beauty and the beauty of the language which clothes them in light.

Do not read this book until you may be alone with it and free to think of it when you have done. It will weary you; not with any weariness of the mind, for it is as exciting as wine or the air of high altitudes, but because you will feel when you have finished it that you have climbed a cloud and that the breath has gone out of your body on the steep ascent. I wish it might be my privilege to retire for a week into a good monastery or a cavern in the side of a hill, there to sleep and wake to a small supper of locusts and wild honey before I should emerge to write this testament. For me this cannot be, but at least you may benefit by my experience; by no means read this book until you have a space of clear leisure about you. Only, as you value your mortal happiness, do not delay too long in scooping that clear cave of leisure out of the surrounding hours, for you must not deny yourself the joy of this book by one unnecessary moment.

I have heard it said by a wise man that this book and "Ulysses" are the two true masterpieces of modern Irish literature. But I have also heard it said by a woman sufficiently wise—if indeed women can ever be wise—that "Ulysses" can be understood only by Dubliners, and by them but imperfectly at times. This gives me a baffled feeling, because I know only too well that I was born in a certain Somerset Country not far from New York and that my father's people came from another Somerset Country in England, which makes me a Saxo-American as ever was. So I have always taken it for granted that I could never understand "Ulysses," and I believe precisely the same sad thing of all the poor young men who have dyed themselves so deeply in the imperial stain of this rare foreign murex. They can imitate Mr. Joyce a little, they can industriously dab themselves with the queer color of his prose, as if the blue murex were woad and they were ancient Britons instead of modern Americans. But, or so I am told, they don't really know what Mr. Joyce has fished up out of the depths of his mind.

Now, here is another sort of book entirely, and the beauty of it is that nobody on earth can imitate it and every one worth his salt can understand it. Homer might have written such a book in the wisdom of his blindness, or Shelley if he had lived to be sixty and ceased to be persecuted, even by his own soul. The one would have been in Greek and the other in an English grown tall enough to stand beside Prometheus, but neither would have belonged to any narrow land or time or people. We should have shared them together like a consecrated bread, just as a hungry German may eat the substance of Shakespeare and be strengthened by it for all the jeers of Shakespeare's loyal countrymen. This is the sort of book to write, if one has the God-given power; this book is a free gift to all minds worthy of it. Even if Mr. Yeats would not choose it to be so, he could not withhold the beauty of this book from a single person who possessed a certain spiritual grace and the power to buy, borrow, or steal, a copy of it.

So far as imitating goes, the thing is quite impossible, for which heaven be praised. Heaven, although I named it idly, is the proper place to praise for giving Mr. Yeats a manner of writing which will not easily encourage imitators. He has a manner, and that manner is, in the good sense, grand; he has few mannerisms, those alluring baby murexes which tempt the fishers of great men. The exquisite simplicity of his prose is solemn and pure; "the fascination of what's difficult" may lure us to lag along behind him; few of us will catch up with him. If I may be permitted one of those paradoxes which Englishmen call bulls and believe to be mistakes, most of the people who could catch up with him have gone before, "to sup with Landor and with Donne."

This art is no miracle, after all; a sentence like this, from "The Trembling of the Veil," is charmingly significant: "When in my twenty-second year I had finished 'The Wanderings of Usheen,' my style seemed too ornamental, too elaborate, and I thought for some weeks of sleeping upon a board." Here is a young person who is taking his work very seriously. I hope it is not a serious fault in myself that I must smile at this; I do not smile in mockery but in delighted memory of kindred impulses of my youth. The book is full of such things; it is a beautiful intensification and heightening of the mental ecstasies and despairs of every artist. In it any one of us who has lived even half as long as Mr. Yeats may read his own spiritual autobiography, enriched and ennobled by a stranger scene and a higher talent, which here springs up into genius.

Only one other autobiographical book, setting aside the published letters of a few poets, has moved me and exalted me as this book has done. That other book was marvelously removed from this, as indeed it seemed to me removed from all life but its Arcadian own. That book, which stands like a solitary golden tree in recollection, was W. H. Hudson's "Far Away and Long Ago." I read it first when I had recovered from what was all but actual death; I was coward enough to distrust my love for it a little, to half believe that it was my own unnaturally sensitive perceptions which made it live so clearly in my mind and heart. I know now that I was wrong, but it was animating to feel again, as I read the "Reveries" of Mr. Yeats's childhood. Here is the same unreality which is so much more real than reality, the same vision of a new heaven and a new earth which is nevertheless half familiar, which "scarce seemed a vision" when we knew it first. It is the sense of finding some lovely thing forgotten since you were a child; "fallings from us, vanishings." Impossible things to put into words, unless a genius is doing it. These two books are as different in all outward ways as is the Argentine from Ireland; Hudson's book is golden and calm as the Garden of Eden, Yeats's book is sad as a weeping April twilight. Hudson is like a child lying in a trance in the sun and watching small living creatures, birds and snakes, moving in a haze of warmth. Yeats, in his "Reveries," is like a child lying in the moonlight and crying mysteriously, yet each is full of enchantment, and each confers a peculiar peace by reason of its beauty. It seems strange that the happy child should have died at last in a poor lodging house and the unhappy child should now be a senator.

It is impossible within the limits of this paper to convey the palest impression of the amazing richness and variety of the later chapters of the book. Never was such a story set down in such a manner; it is too good to be true long after you have finished, and yet you know it is true. When Keats heard that a gold ring of Anne Hathaway's had been found in a field at Stratford-on-Avon, he wrote to a friend, "I shall go mad!" I have felt this precise incredulous ecstasy at moments when I beheld some word or thing which seemed too wonderful to be true; there are stories in this book which so affect my spirits. Like Keats, I imagine for an instant that I shall go mad. This I feel when I see, through language transparent as a sheet of crystal, the proud and touching figure of Lionel Johnson proceed to his doom. I have always loved this lonely and incredibly distinguished creature, not only for his delicate and bitter verse, but for his virtues and defects as I knew them from slight, inadequate accounts. Now I have him before me as clearly as if Mr. Yeats's Christian Cabbala had been potent to summon him from his grave. The picture of the rooms in Charlotte Street, with the gray corduroy curtains and the innumerable bookshelves and the elegant, scornful, fanatical little Lionel reading all night because he could not sleep; this is as I had imagined it, and now that I truly see it it is like something foreknown in a dream. "Talking there by candlelight it never seemed very difficult to murmur Villiers de l'Isle Adam's proud words, 'As for living—our servants will do that for us.' Yet I can now see that Johnson himself in some half-conscious part of him desired the world he had renounced." Small wonder; it must have been sad to live alone with a dark angel.

The tale of the Rhymers Club is so tragic that only its vast excitement makes it bearable. Dowson and Davidson and Lionel Johnson himself all came to cruel ends; it is to be presumed that the gods loved them, especially the two younger. I am glad to know one delightful story of the scholarly Lionel; I think I like it even better than "Morfydd." He said once to Yeats: "One should use a colon where other people use a semicolon, and semicolon where other people use a comma." He would of course always say precisely that, and how I love him for it!

The account of Oscar Wilde and the tragedy of his ruin is extraordinary. Here for the first time I have been able to see a dignity behind the horror; Mr. Yeats has unsealed my eyes and made me more generous and more just. "'Wilde will never lift his head again,' said the art critic, Gleeson White, 'for he has against him all men of infamous life.' When the verdict was announced the harlots in the street outside danced upon the pavement."

Aubrey Beardsley, dragged down by Wilde's destruction through no fault of his own, save that he was unpopular and it was "the moment for getting rid of unpopular people"; Henley, like a wounded lion after the death of his little girl; John Synge–these names make it indeed "The Tragic Generation"! Of Synge Mr. Yeats has a wise and profound saying, which I will quote for the pleasure it gives me:

"No mind can engender till divided into two, but that of a Keats or a Shelley falls into an intellectual part that follows and a hidden emotional flying image, whereas in a mind like that of Synge the emotional part is dreaded and stagnant, while the intellectual part is a clear mirror-like technical achievement."

This book is as much for painters as poets; the stories of the Pre-Raphaelites of Bedford Park, of Morris and the eccentric Nettleship are all of an extreme fascination. The figure of Maude Gonne seems itself like a painting by a true Pre-Raphaelite; it has the early innocence of art. I suppose it is most of all like a statue of gold and ivory made by the elder, which is to say the younger, Greeks. This is a noble creature; my heart does not warm to her as it does to the red-haired girl of good family who was so poor that she lived on a pennyworth of bread and cocoa shells a day and yet hired a woman to go with her to the art school, because she did not think that a lady should walk in the street alone. But it is all the fabric of romance; there is not a page which fails to shine with some peculiar light.

I suppose I must find a flaw or two–no emerald is real without them. I might say, and truly, that sometimes I do not very much like Mr. Yeats himself; he seems very solemn and very selfish at times. But then this makes it all so much truer and gives me the excuse that I want, to say that as I read I have often seen myself in this far greater artist, and that I believe every one who reads the book will in some measure see the image of himself in its crystal.

Jewelled Bindings

New Republic, December 5, 1923
Collected Prose of Elinor Wylie. New York: Alfred A. Knopf, 1933

I have purloined my title, as I am fond of doing, from the literary imagination of another, to whom my thanks are hereby offered. John Webster furnished me with Nets to Catch the Wind; I took Black Armour from Lionel Johnson; to the anonymous author of an announcement of a sale at the Anderson galleries I am indebted for this present caption. The phrase, as it originally stood upon the pages of a fairly prominent review, was Superb Jewelled Bindings, but I am forced to let the sumptuous qualification go the way of all too many brave things, and thus sink into oblivion. The bindings of which I propose to write are hardly superb; they are elaborate, neat, enamelled, elegant, perhaps exquisite, but they lack the vast suavity of the truly superb in art. They are the bindings, the spiritual bonds, the sharp and delicately turned shapes and forms which so decoratively constrict the essence of contemporary lyric verse.

Permit me to quote from the picturesque bit of prose whence my title was stolen. "Surrounding this is a large wreath of laurel, tied with a mauve ribbon, and studded with fifty-eight pearls set in gold. Disposed around the cover are two hundred and twenty-three garnets and four opals. The design of the back cover is equally brilliant and contains forty-eight garnets, eight opals, eight moonstones, twenty-eight turquoises, twelve blue chalcedonies, two hundred and fifty-four amethysts, and nine topazes. There are scores of similar bindings, elaborate in design and lavish in the use of precious stones."

Surrounding what? you may well ask. At the Anderson Galleries all this intricacy surrounds Some Poems by John Keats, but in the curious museum of our own time some, nay many, poems by eminent young lyricists appear, if not similarly tied with mauve ribbon, at least painstakingly inlaid with seven moonstones and twelve blue chalcedonies. The large laurel wreath, though it has not yet been permanently awarded, has been bespoke by several, and he is poor indeed who cannot afford a few garnets and amethysts, or a mild fresh-water pearl.

So I figure us to myself, dwindled to the jewel brightness of the picture in a camera obscura, hunched over our filing and fitting, careful lapidaries, clever goldsmiths, excellent workmen for the most part, but a thought too intent upon the binding. Of course there are obvious exceptions; your personal predilections will supply their names. If I hesitate to say that I am one of the chief offenders, it is only because a writer's claim to distinction, even in crime, annoys the intelligent reader. So—bowing always in the direction of the obvious exceptions—let me refer to us as a group, enchanted by a midas-touch or a colder silver madness into workers in metal and glass, in substances hard and brittle, in crisp and sharp-edged forms. From this company I exclude all persons whose poetry the Dial will publish, whether their lines rhyme or no. I include only the lyric poets, more or less young, entirely modern, who are, among a hundred and something million Americans, leaving little verse unto that enormous clan.

When I say little, I mean literally diminutive; short lines, clear small stanzas, brilliant and compact. I don't mean inferior or contemptible or negligible. Neither do I mean great.

One of the most enchanting conceits of the eighteenth century was the enamelled snuff-box, which opened to reveal not brown tobacco dust but a bright and singing bird. And although some few of our modern boxes have nothing but powdery dryness under their neat painted lids, most of them are music-boxes, whose gilded birds repeat a fine variety of tunes, melodious, bitter, passionate, or intellectual, as the case may be. And for this sort of singing a small jewelled receptacle of two or three well-polished stanzas is no bad thing; it is comfortable and fitting. Did I suspect for a moment, as in my own case I have not dared to suspect, that my bird was a live one, I should let him out.

I should let him out into freedom, but not necessarily into free verse. I should try to remember that he was born in a snuff-box, and be prepared to build him another house, a stone dovecote or a wicker cage, according to his nature. I should let him perch in the groves of Academe if he liked, or upon a bramble bush of ballads. If he were a real bird he would know his own mind, and his own music.

But the question remains unanswered, in my opinion at least, as to whether we have shut up any eagles or nightingales in our snuff-boxes. And I believe we are good workmen, dexterous and clean in our handling of gold and silver and precious–or even semi-precious–stones. I believe we are careful and conscientious, but not so much so as our detractors declare. I think rather that we have found a manner which very justly encloses our matter, a letter which very nicely defines our spirit. As to the decoration, the setting of words transparent or opaque in a pattern upon our jewelled bindings, I am by no means ready to discard it. It is a deliberate art, perhaps, but as such it is a discipline and a struggle not to be too impetuously scorned. If our spirit is greater than the thing that holds it, it will go free of its own accord; our work is notoriously brittle, and I have no fear that its forms will ever imprison an authentic genius. And, in the remote possibility that some of us are not geniuses, but only adroit and talented young people with a passion for writing verse, it may be an excellent thing after all that we have cultivated a small clean technique. A number of minor poets are far better employed in being brittle and bright and metallic than in being soft and opulently luscious. It keeps the workshop tidier, and leaves a little elbow-room in which the very great may move their hammers and chisels in serenity.

Symbols in Literature

English Journal, June 1928
Collected Prose of Elinor Wylie. New York: Alfred A. Knopf, 1933

There was once an apocryphal German professor who proposed an amended version of certain lines from *As You Like It.* Shakespeare, he suggested, had drunk rather too much canary or Rhenish when he wrote, "Sermons in stones, books in the running brooks." It should obviously, said the Herr Professor, be reversed; sermons belonged in books and stones were frequently found in brooks. And this is true enough, as any mere clergyman or geologist can affirm, and yet it is not half so true as the thing Shakespeare said.

In another book, even greater than *As You Like It,* there is a prolonged and consistent use of parables. When, in the 80th Psalm, the history of Israel is compared to the growth of a vine, the device of metaphor is magnificently successful. If you dislike a rich man, and find it hard to believe that he will ever go to heaven, you will think of the eye of a needle even quicker than you will think of Dives. The Unwise Virgin is so present an image in every one's mind that it is possible to-day to call a play *Behold the Bridegroom* and make your meaning plain to the population of Broadway.

Therefore I do not, in this paper, intend to apologize for allegories. I believe that no single person who reads my words has not accepted allegories as the very essence of truth, and grown so familiar with that truth that he has forgotten that they were allegories. It is simply that in the older stories, the ones which have become part not only of our literature but of our lives, the symbol has become a name for the thing itself, the mask is immediately recognized. Perhaps it is not accurate nowadays to say that every one will immediately recognize Punch and Judy as a wife-beater and a shrew, but certainly every one will recognize Charlie Chaplin as a tragic clown and Mary Pickford as a good little girl. If the most literal-minded person among us wishes to describe a man whose generosity passes the bounds of worldly wisdom, he will not cast his mind's eye up and down Main Street for a comparison; he will say that the man is quixotic, and all his literal and realistic friends will accept that word as descriptive. In every circus traveling over the dusty length and breadth of the American summer, the dwarfs will be called Lilliputians, and all the little children will understand quite well that they are not giants. It is too much to expect of the average person to remember that these words came from the bitter and brilliant allegories of Cervantes and Swift, but I ask the readers of this paper to remember it, and to marvel at the lasting power of the symbolical in art.

I wish to avoid the word "fantasy"; it reminds too many people of Dr. Freud of Vienna, and it reminds me of those blithe patterns upon printed silks which the French call *fantaisie*. It is not a word of sufficient dignity and worth to describe *The Fairie Queene*, or *Pilgrim's Progress*, or *Gulliver's Travels*. It is not a word of sufficient dignity and worth to describe *The Faerie Queene*, or *Pilgrim's Progress*, or *Gulliver's Travels*. I myself should hesitate to apply it to *Lady into Fox*; certainly it is not a noble enough name for *Mr. Weston's Good Wine*. These things are all allegories, of less or greater merit and grandeur; some are slight, and some are heroic, but they are all too good to be called fantasies.

Now the literal-minded may ask—or so I am credibly informed—why Mr. Bunyan did not tell the realistic story of a persecuted dissenter, and why Mr. Powys did not tell the naturalistic tale of an English village. But for some unknown reason he will ask this question more indignantly in the case of Mr. Powys than in the case of Mr. Bunyan, for to many people it seems forgivable to be allegorical in the seventeenth century and excessively foolish to be allegorical in the twentieth. I think, although it is impossible to be sure about anything so mysterious as this theory, that the explanation is quite simple; to the literal minded, Mr. Bunyan's real history is very nearly as fantastic as the story of Christian's pilgrimage, and the steel helmet of the Parliamentary soldier as strange as Christian's staff and scrip. Whereas Mr. Powys lives to-day, and recognizes the existence of Fords and Woolworth Stores, and these things should disinfect a man's imagination against all danger of visions. Only, thank God, they don't, and if you stop to think of it, Mr. Bunyan's flintlock probably seemed as prosaic and modern to him as Mr. Powys's umbrella undoubtedly seems to Mr. Powys. In the same way, Mr. Literal-Minded really sees very little difference between the court of Queen Anne and the court of Brobdignag, and he thinks the Rev. Dean Swift quite justified in being savage and insanely fanciful about politics and morals. He wishes, however—or so I am credibly informed—that modern writers would be sensibly modern, and stick to their Gopher Prairies and their American Tragedies.

Now as a matter of cold fact, both Mr. Lewis's books and the even more amazing books of Mr. Dreiser are full of allegorical figures. Over the books of Mr. Dreiser there broods a terrific figure of blind and tragic Chance, blinder by far than Mr. Hardy's Chance, who did after all in the final analysis belong to the Church of England. Mr. Dreiser's Chance is a sort of Cyclops with his eye put out; he frightens Mr. Dreiser more than the Cyclops ever frightened Ulysses. As for Mr. Lewis, his Babbitt is one of the lesser gods of the American mythology;

he is a mere metaphor. He is really no more realistic than Gargantua, though he is not nearly so lovable.

I admit, however, that these gentlemen are not meaning to write allegories. They are doing it in spite of themselves, and against all their principles and convictions. Among those who are speaking in parables and violating no principles in so doing, the most distinguished examples are Mr. T. F. Powys, Mr. David Garnett, and Miss Sylvia Townsend Warner. In the books of these three English writers, the events of the story are sometimes supernatural; the forces of the universe of good and evil, the common courses of nature are changed and twisted into miracles and portents. The same thing happens in any fairy story; it happens in Cinderella and in Little Red Riding Hood. But this is no reason for laughing at these books, or for stupidly wondering; the same thing happens in Homer's *Odyssey* and in *Hamlet*. There is even an element of the supernatural in the Bible, and the best critics do not hold that the power and majesty of that book is lessened thereby.

Another and less clearly defined form of allegory is that in which the story is possible, but frankly improbable and strange. In this class belong many books of adventure; whether the writer knew it or not, I believe that a writer has seldom assumed a toga or a periwig save as a mask or disguise for his deeper meaning. I am not, of course, speaking of the ruck of historical novels, but I think I see Mr. Thackeray's blacker moods dressed up as Esmond, and Stevenson happily escaping with Jim Hawkins. Into this class I put my own books, with the single exception of the *Venetian Glass Nephew,* which contains a light hint of the supernatural, perfectly susceptible of being explained away by the sober-minded.

Now why should anyone wish to wear a pair of wings or a periwig, and pretend to be an angel or a *chevalier d'industrie?* The answer is somewhat complicated, but nowhere has it been more happily expressed than in a short essay by Mr. Christopher Morley, dealing with a brief allegorical novel of several years ago which Mr. Morley was kind enough to admire. I will quote his opening paragraph,

> There are always excellent reasons for silence. One worthy reason is that you have nothing to say. Another that what you are thinking is too important to be said, or would become untrue if uttered. The recourse of those who feel that they have something to say, but desire to avoid the bitterness of being understood, has been (ever since Aesop) the fable of fantasy. The importance of any fable can be gauged by the area of silence it covers. Abraham Lincoln, a very Aesopian person, could conceal the whole blackness of Civil War in an anecdote.

That is excellent and exact. "To avoid the bitterness of being understood"– that holds good for the mighty Swift, although it was written about one of the least of the allegorists of this generation. And to avoid the bitterness of understanding; sometimes it is that. And to be able to put a red beard or a lion's skin on your worst enemy, or to seize a rapier or an old-fashioned squirrel rifle, and have at them without explanation or apology. If Swift had written about the king's mistresses he would have been imprisoned, but by calling them cushions he could be as bitter as he pleased, or very nearly, for nobody was ever so bitter as the Dean pleased. If you call a spade a diamond some people will think you are frivolous and affected, but other people will understand how much blacker things may be said about spades by the simple trick of pretending that they are diamonds.

Index of First Lines